Secrets to Get Organized in Minutes

Quick and easy ways to save time and simplify your life!

By Alex A. Lluch
Author of over 3 million books sold!

WS Publishing Group
www.WSPublishingGroup.com
San Diego, California 92119

Secrets to Get Organized in Minutes

By Alex A. Lluch

Published by WS Publishing Group
San Diego, California 92119
Copyright © 2009 by WS Publishing Group

Designed by WS Publishing Group:
David Defenbaugh and Sarah Jang

Image Credits:

Cover image © iStockphoto/Christoph Ermel

pg.5 © iStockphoto/Koksharov Dmitry
pg. 9 © iStockphoto/Narvikk
pg. 51 © iStockphoto/Ivan Stevanovic
pg. 117 © iStockphoto/Luis Carlos Torres
pg. 147 © iStockphoto/Ivan Stevanovic
pg. 189 © iStockphoto/Ivan Stevanovic

icons © iStockphoto/Lushik:
pg. 10, calendar, moving truck
pg. 118, stamp, money
pg. 148, internet symbol, wallet, box

icons © iStockphoto/Scottdunlap:
pg. 10, clipboard
pg. 52, pencil, house, tool box
pg. 118, chart

For Inquiries:
Log on to www.WSPublishingGroup.com
E-mail info@WSPublishingGroup.com

ISBN-13: 978-1-934386-42-2

Printed in China

Introduction

Organize
your life!

Everyone can use some help getting organized. Case in point, Thomas Alva Edison is credited with developing the light bulb, phonograph, and many other devices that contributed to modern cinema and telecommunications. His thirst for knowledge fueled his genius and kept him working around the clock for many years. Edison was also famously disorganized—he constantly took notes on his discoveries, then left them lying around in his laboratory. As his inventions garnered attention, he realized he needed a system for organizing his work. However, he was much too busy inventing to do the job himself.

Edison enlisted assistants to tackle the monumental job of organizing his documents, notes, sketches, and plans. In 1877, he even banned the use of loose papers in his lab and began to record his notes in notebooks. Still, papers were misplaced, misfiled, and many simply disappeared. Edison finally hired a full-time secretary to organize his work but everything prior to this move was in hopeless disarray—as is evidenced by the collection of more than 5 million papers housed at the Edison National Historic Site in West Orange, New Jersey.

Like Edison, there are millions of smart, talented, and capable Americans who require outside help to get their lives organized. The tips included in *Secrets to Get Organized in Minutes* are for people of all vocations and lifestyles who simply need a bit of inspiration and guidance. *Secrets to Get Organized in Minutes* contains everything you need to get—and stay—organized. This book offers you innovative suggestions for organizing every aspect of your life. Daily, monthly, and yearly checklists help you stay organized once you have put in all the hard work and dedication.

organize your thoughts

Let your first order of business be to organize your thoughts. Start by making a list of how organizing everything from your calendar to your closet will make your life easier.

Consider how organizing your life, time, important documents, finances, and possessions will impact your daily life. Imagine having a system in place to deal with scheduling conflicts, incoming mail, and the accumulation of debt. Ponder what it must feel like to save time and money—as well as significantly reduce your stress level—by knowing exactly where to find what you need. These are just some of the topics covered in *Secrets to Get Organized in Minutes*.

By following the tips in this book you will learn to develop your own brilliant system for organizing your life and your possessions!

Life & Time

In this
section

Priorities

Come up with a list of daily, weekly, and monthly priorities. Laying out your objectives offers you a timeline in which to accomplish your goals. It also highlights your main priorities and reveals recurring interests and themes.

quick start tip

Decide on a Top 5

Make a "Top 5" list of the key components that make up your life. An example of a Top 5 list might include, "Connect with spouse; spend time with kids; focus on career; pursue education; nurture hobbies." When drafting your list, prevent overlap. Once you've identified the key areas of your life, commit to giving each component your full and undivided attention.

Make a timeframe
for your big picture

Prioritizing starts with creating a timeframe to help you reach your big-picture goals. Identify what these are: "Getting an advanced degree" or "Opening a restaurant" are good examples. Set up checklists to help evaluate your progress. Making gains toward a larger purpose will help you feel in control of your life. As a result, you will be less susceptible to distractions and be more organized.

➔ Dedicate 75 percent of your time to your Top 5

Keep track of your activities for one week, marking down how long it takes to complete each task. Make sure to write down everything you do but specially note activities that fall into one of your Top 5 priorities. Next, note whether more than 25 percent of your time is taken up by tasks that do not support your Top 5. If so, narrow your focus and change your schedule accordingly. Your goal is to spend the majority of your time on the activities and goals that are most important to you.

Put your loved ones first

Workaholics spend more time at the office than with their friends and family, believing that the people in their lives will be there when "things settle down." But intending to spend time with a loved one is not the same as actually doing it. Too often, our loved ones are no longer around by the time we have free time. Avoid this fate by making a balanced work-family life a top priority of yours. Carve out time each day to maintain your closest relationships.

Take 30 minutes to get fit

The National Institutes of Health recommends that adults engage in moderate exercise, such as swimming, walking, hiking, dancing, or cycling 5 times a week for 30 minutes. There are 1,440 minutes in each day—surely you can set aside 30 of those to optimize your health and reduce stress, both of which improve your mood and productivity.

Try This!

Learn to say "no." It's important! Doing favors and making commitments is nice once in awhile. But saying "yes" too often forces you to frequently say "no" to your own needs. Practice saying "no" to all but the most important events and note how much extra time you have to spend on what really counts!

Keep It Organized

NOW

❏ Make a list of your important people and make time for them
❏ Commit to working a 40-hour week, no more, no less
❏ Evaluate how you feel as you perform your daily activities
❏ List goals you would like to accomplish within the next year

MONTHLY

❏ Revisit your Top 5 list to see if your priorities are still the same
❏ Call an old friend and catch up
❏ Ask your partner out on a date
❏ Take stock of—and celebrate—accomplishments

YEARLY

❏ Make a new list of your Top 5 priorities
❏ Plan a trip
❏ Identify your core values and consider how closely you stick to them
❏ Ask yourself if your big picture still fits

Calendar

An updated calendar organizes your work, social, and family engagements. Calendars do more than remind you to prepare for important meetings, birthdays, and anniversaries. They help you evaluate how you spend your time. Use one so you don't get to the end of your week wondering where the time went.

quick start tip

Combine your calendars

Having separate calendars for home and work wastes time and inevitably leads to scheduling conflicts. For many of us, work and home are so intertwined it makes sense to keep one comprehensive schedule of events. Consult it before making any commitments and have it on hand to prevent over-scheduling, double-booking, and other time-wasting mistakes.

Put your
calendar online

Most people are able to use the Internet just about anywhere. With such widespread access, keeping an online calendar is a fast and efficient way to immediately organize your events. Programs such as Microsoft Outlook and Google Calendar allow you to sync events directly to your calendar by simply clicking on an icon. Google Calendar also allows you to create several different calendars that can be synced to each other or be shared with coworkers and family.

⊕ Carry a day planner

For those who prefer a hard copy calendar, invest in a day planner. Choose a planner with enough space to match your busy lifestyle—but make sure it is also compact enough to take with you everywhere you go. Also, choose a planner that suits your style, so you become more likely to use it. For at-a-glance purposes, use a red pencil to note work-related activities, a blue one for personal commitments, and a green one for family dates.

Enter birthdays
and anniversaries

Don't be the guy who forgets his anniversary or the girl who forgets her friend's birthday! Prepare for all significant celebrations by entering every important date you can think of for the entire year as soon as you start a new calendar. Update it as necessary and consult it often. Planning ahead has its perks—such as having plenty of time to plan a great party and choose the perfect gift. Online tools like www.birthdayalarm.com can get you started.

Record exercise on your calendar

Many people feel like they don't have time for exercise, but you can schedule 30 minutes or more a few days a week if you write it down on your calendar. Mark off the days when you exercise and you will begin to enjoy the look of a week full of workouts. Soon enough, this becomes a habit. Building time for exercise on your calendar means organizing your week to make room for your health and sanity.

Try This!

Create a master calendar for your home. Hang a large dry erase calendar in a room where family congregates. Ask each member of your family to write their schedule on the calendar. Assign each person their own color marker so events and conflicts are clear.

Keep It Organized

NOW

☐ Write due dates for all your bills on your calendar
☐ Email friends and family to ask for their birthdays
☐ Set habitual events such as weekly meetings to recur in your calendar
☐ Pencil in time each day to relax or do nothing
☐ Mark or X out the days when you exercise and write what you did

MONTHLY

☐ Write in important developments like weddings and trips
☐ Choose a date by which to accomplish a specific goal
☐ Create a realistic exercise schedule for the upcoming month
☐ Evaluate the accuracy of your calendar and make necessary changes

YEARLY

☐ Start a new online calendar
☐ Jot down some long-term goals you want to accomplish
☐ Buy a new day planner or refills for the one you already have
☐ Have personalized calendars made up for loved ones

Daily Schedule

Creating a daily schedule is an easy way to organize your time. Without it, each day starts as a blank slate that you scramble to fill with different activities. Starting your day with a planned agenda gives each day a theme and you a sense of purpose.

quick start tip

Become a master list maker

Before you go to bed, make a list of tasks you must accomplish the following day. Include every conceivable activity—from going to the gym to mailing the rent to grocery shopping to projects at work. When you wake up, you will have a road map of what you need to accomplish. Cross off each item as you complete it and carry unfinished tasks over to the next day.

Spice up your
daily agenda

Days that drudge along are usually the ones filled with too many mundane tasks. When creating your daily agenda, pepper it with activities you enjoy, too—such as dinner with a friend, time to read a "for fun" book, or a lunchtime rendezvous with your partner. Make sure every daily agenda has at least one thing you really want to do.

⊃ Include "nonnegotiables" in your daily schedule

When time is an issue, the first thing most people give up is exercise, healthy eating habits, and much-needed down time. Ironically, skipping these habits causes us to feel even more worn down and frazzled. It is important, then, to build these items into your daily schedule. Treat them as "nonnegotiable" events, as set in stone as a meeting with your boss or a doctor's appointment. Through these nonnegotiables you will establish "me time" and offer yourself a sense of order, even in the most chaotic of times.

Create a buffer zone
around daily activities

Everyone encounters a traffic accident or spills coffee on their lap now and then. Stacking activities one after the other with no buffer zone only adds to the stress of these situations. Instead, build time around each activity on your agenda to allow for unexpected interruptions. Doing so will help prevent the domino effect of having your entire schedule thrown off. Having time between appointments or tasks also allows for additional preparation and relaxation.

Avoid going rogue! Stick to your daily agenda

The whole point of creating a daily schedule is to give your day structure. So, avoid the temptation to improvise or change it on a whim! Do as directors advise their actors and "stick to the script." Let your schedule serve its purpose as your guide to the day. In doing so you will successfully achieve time management and organization.

Try This!

Use a dry erase board to map out your day. Writing out your agenda on a large, erasable surface is a great way to "think out loud." Organize tasks into 3 columns labeled Must, Should, and Would Like To. Include in your schedule a variety of tasks from each category.

Keep It Organized

NOW

❏ Keep a notebook on your nightstand to write down midnight ideas
❏ Make a small list of nonnegotiable daily activities that are just for you
❏ Carry your planner with you to make adjustments to your agenda
❏ Include a mix of work, family, and social events in your daily schedule

MONTHLY

❏ Recycle or shred the previous month's lists to avoid accumulating clutter
❏ Evaluate the effectiveness of your list-making abilities
❏ Add events to your daily schedule
❏ Celebrate your scheduling skills with a "free" day that has no planned activities

YEARLY

❏ Purchase a new dry erase board and markers
❏ Evaluate how much smoother your days have been since becoming a list maker!

Family Schedule

Create a comprehensive calendar that includes the entire family. Include children! Having kids participate is an excellent way to develop their time management and organizational skills. It also teaches them to honor commitments and respect others' time.

quick start tip

Ask your kids about their weekly commitments

Keep track of your children's whereabouts by asking them to make you a weekly list of their activities. Tell them to include birthday parties, study groups, music lessons, soccer games, and any event that occurs outside of school hours. This lets you know what your kids are up to as well as highlights the best time for family activities.

Ask coaches to
email team schedules

Kids who play sports are constantly on the go and thus, tend to be disorganized. Somewhere in a backpack full of books and sports equipment is the team schedule for practices and games, but who wants to rummage through that mess to find out when a game is? Rather than relying on your child, ask his or her coach to email you a season schedule—and then show up to cheer.

→ Eat family dinner together

The television show *The Gilmore Girls* made famous "Dreaded Friday Night Family Dinners." Like these witty mother-daughter characters, your kids will likely fight forced family time. However, they will accept it eventually if it is scheduled and consistent.

Do your best to make family dinner fun by planning meals your kids love. Involve them in the planning and let them rotate nights they get to pick what is cooked. Be willing to serve food that is a little on the indulgent side—after all, their faces around the dinner table are what's most important.

Establish a regular date night

A study conducted by Ohio State University found that couples spend just one-third of their time together after having a child. One way to correct this imbalance is to carve out adult-only time with your partner. Choose one day of the week for dinner out, drinks, or a movie—anything that interests you and gets you out of the house together. Once scheduled, do not let anything but an emergency derail your date.

Check the school calendar

Adding school events to your already busy lifestyle can get hairy—especially with no notice. Check out events in advance on your child's school website—most schools now put their calendar of events online. Consult it and note any PTA meetings, school plays, concerts, or fundraisers that interest you, and make a point to attend.

Try This!

The best families are democracies, not dictatorships. When conflicts arise with your family calendar, take a family vote on making changes to it. It is important to respect family time, but everyone should be able to truly be there. If you do have to cancel family time, reschedule it immediately.

Keep It Organized

NOW

❑ Set aside 30 minutes each week for family scheduling
❑ Create a shared online calendar and set up email reminders
❑ Make "free passes" on index cards and give 1 per month to each family member—these can be used to get out of a commitment
❑ Creating a walking/feeding schedule for pets

MONTHLY

❑ Give out organization awards to children who stick to the family calendar
❑ Schedule a family outing
❑ At the start of each month, go over your family calendar for that month (but serve your family ice cream at the meeting!)
❑ Evaluate whether your children's schedules are too demanding

YEARLY

❑ Let the kids pick out their own personal calendars
❑ Buy a family calendar the whole family likes

Parties

Planning parties can either be fun and satisfying or stressful and disappointing. Getting organized is the key to making your experience one or the other. It is rare that a party springs out of nowhere, and there are plenty of ways to prepare.

quick start tip

Keep your ideas in a Party Box

With each party you learn something. Jot these lessons down and put them in a designated Party Box. Whether it's food-to-person ratios, when to put icing on cupcakes, or a brilliant idea for party favors, collecting these little tidbits saves time and money by preventing you from making the same mistake twice.

Form a party
planning committee

Planning is more fun when you do it with others. Since most of the milestones you celebrate will be with your immediate circle, it can be fun to join forces with friends to party plan and combine resources. Once you enlist a few people to help, designate people to be in charge of certain tasks—and most importantly, have fun when you get together to plan!

➔ Get green invitations

Eco-friendly invitations are an easy way to bring a conscience to your celebration. There are several ways to go green. You can purchase invitations printed on recycled paper, hunt for vintage invites in thrift stores, or create online invitations using websites like Evite.com.

That Evite is paperless is just one of its advantages. Other perks include having an immediate online record of those invited and whether they will attend. You can also include location links, maps, directions, and phone numbers, and have the power to email people who haven't yet RSVP'd.

Build parties
around a theme

The greatest parties are built around a theme. Learn what the celebrated person enjoys and then create a party around those interests. For example, throwing a popstar-themed birthday party for a 12-year-old girl—complete with a karaoke machine stocked with the star's songs—is sure to keep the girls giggling for hours. Themes work for adults, too. Having a clear focus is not only fun and creative, it also makes party planning a snap. A theme helps narrow down your choices for decorations, favors, and other party touches.

Establish a Party Closet

Don't throw out leftover party hats, noise makers, or plastic cups! Store them for next time in labeled plastic containers in a designated party closet. If you can't devote a full closet, carve out space on a few shelves—or use a big storage bin. Keeping party supplies in one spot makes it easy to evaluate what you need for your next bash.

Try This!

When planning a party, delegate duties to avoid becoming overwhelmed. Ask volunteers to be in charge of one component of the party—food, drinks, dessert, entertainment, etc. If the party is for your partner, give small jobs to your kids so they are in on the planning.

Keep It Organized

NOW

❑ Make a list of events worth celebrating over the next year
❑ Create a spreadsheet with addresses, phone numbers, and email addresses
❑ Collect interesting stamps to put on special invitations
❑ Create playlists on your computer so you have music ready to go

MONTHLY

❑ Check your party supplies and replenish as necessary
❑ Invite friends over for a dinner party
❑ Wash, fold, and iron cloth napkins and table cloths
❑ Try a few new recipes and file them for future use

YEARLY

❑ Stock up on thank you cards
❑ Begin planning at least one large party—such as New Year's Eve, Fourth of July, or a wedding anniversary

Vacation

Lay the groundwork for your next trip at least 6 months in advance. This gives you plenty of time to save, research destinations, and keep an eye on fluctuating airfares. Take your time and remember that planning a vacation is half the fun!

quick start tip

Decide whether to go big or small

What type of vacation do you prefer? Several restful, three-day-weekend trips, or an exotic adventure that lasts several weeks? Choose early in the year whether you would like to take one big vacation or several small getaways. Doing so will shape your other vacation-related decisions—from destination, to budget, to time off, to luggage.

Open a
coffee can account

Establish a travel fund and start saving for your next trip. Put a minimum of $5 to $10 each week in a coffee can—more when you can afford to. Toss all spare change in it—especially quarters—and don't touch this money until you are ready to go. Use funds in the coffee can to supplement your spending budget when you arrive at your destination. Saving $10 a week for 6 months adds $240 to your fund for your next trip!

⊃ Collect destination stories and reviews

Some of the best ideas for a trip come from others' stories, so pay attention and start collecting ideas.

Invite a friend over who just returned from an exotic destination and pick her brain for details. Take notes and keep them in a travel file. Clip articles from travel magazines that interest you. Visit online travel review sites, such as Tripadvisor.com, and print out any noteworthy reviews. Put these together in a small, handy binder that you can carry with you while traveling.

Sign up to receive
travel deal emails

All major airlines, hotels, and car rental agencies offer travel deals to those who book online. Set up accounts with a few of each to receive emails about discounts and packages. Create a "Vacation" folder in your email and file travel emails as they come in to keep them organized. Remember that these deals often have time limits, so set your online calendar to alert you when interesting deals are set to expire.

Conserve vacation days and personal time off

Time is a major obstacle that keeps hard working adults from taking vacation. Many people burn up their paid time off with errands or sick days, and some even let the time go unused. To keep your vacation time for vacations, plan appointments and errands during lunch hours and weekends. Use sick days for doctor visits for you and your kids, and keep at least 5 days in reserve for leisure time.

Try This!

Most travel destinations have peak and off-season rates. Travel off-season whenever possible to save money and beat crowds.
If you do not mind afternoon rainstorms in Costa Rica during summer, or a nippy trip to London in winter, make sure to book your trip during off-season time periods.

Keep It Organized

NOW
- ❏ Make a travel folder
- ❏ Open frequent flyer or rewards accounts with airlines
- ❏ Make a travel budget for the year and start saving
- ❏ Talk with your travel partner about destination ideas

MONTHLY
- ❏ Read through emailed travel deals from airlines and hotels
- ❏ Put an additional $50 in your travel fund
- ❏ Price your entire trip on Priceline.com, Travelocity.com, or Orbitz.com
- ❏ Rent movies that take place in cities you want to visit
- ❏ Check out travel guides from the library

YEARLY
- ❏ Plan your travel calendar for the year
- ❏ Know how many vacation, sick, and personal days you have accrued
- ❏ Learn words and phrases in the language of a country you want to visit

Shopping

Shopping without a list causes people to overspend and forget important items. Save time and money by getting into the habit of writing down what you need before shopping. Organized shoppers know how to create lists, cut costs, save time, and get the best quality for their dollar.

quick start tip

Make a list, and check it twice

Keep a magnetized pad on your freezer or fridge door where you constantly write down depleted household items. Organize items by greatest need and by what kind of store you'll need to get them from (your local organic co-op might be your one-stop shop for veggies, but cleaning supplies might need to come from a traditional grocery store).

Shop for presents
all year long

Don't leave holiday shopping to the last minute, when crowds are thick and products are slim pickings. Instead, keep an eye on sales and shop for gifts all year. Hide your purchased presents in a closet, basement, or garage, and pull from your stash for birthdays, holidays, and other important events—just remember to replenish your gift supply when it runs low.

➲ Carry a coupon wallet

Few things are more frustrating then clipping dozens of coupons only to forget them when you go grocery shopping. Prevent this by keeping coupons and other discount tickets on you at all times.

When you get a coupon, immediately put it in a wallet or small organizer that is for coupons only. Toss it in your purse, canvas shopping bag, or in the glove compartment of your car. Even if you forget about coupons on your way to the store, you'll have them when you get there.

Make a realistic
shopping budget

Shopping without a budget leads to overspending and financial "hangovers." And since nothing feeds disorganization like losing track of one's finances, creating—and sticking to—a shopping budget will keep your organization skills sober and alert. Allocate a certain amount of money from each paycheck to pay for food, clothes, entertainment, and other shopping needs. Combine this budget with the lists you have made for what items your house needs and where you can best get them. You'll feel in charge of spending and reduce the urge to impulse-buy.

Keep canvas bags in your car

Make your shopping trips environmentally friendly by switching to canvas shopping bags. These are better for the environment than plastic or paper bags, and also for your wallet—it is becoming increasingly fashionable for stores to issue a 5-cent credit per bag when you bring your own.

Try This!

Even with lists, we forget important items and double-up on others. Before leaving the house, check the refrigerator, cupboards, pantry, bathroom, and laundry room to see if you missed anything. Add or subtract items as needed to ensure you have an accurate list as well as a stocked home.

Keep It Organized

NOW

- ❏ Set aside one day a week to clip and organize coupons
- ❏ Tell family members to write down their shopping needs, then compare to prevent overlap
- ❏ Ask yourself if you really need it
- ❏ Take stock of what is in your pantry
- ❏ Designate one day a week to do grocery shopping

MONTHLY

- ❏ Take stock of home office supplies that need replenishing
- ❏ Buy stamps when you get cash from an ATM
- ❏ Treat yourself to a $50 shopping trip for sticking to a budget
- ❏ Note what food is wasted and make changes to your grocery list
- ❏ Compare online deals to in-store prices

YEARLY

- ❏ Purchase extended warranties on big-ticket items

Menu Planning

Planning menus a week in advance takes the guesswork out of what to feed your family. Create your own system for collecting recipes, planning meals, shopping for ingredients, and preparing and storing food. Having a plan eliminates time wasted standing in front of an empty refrigerator wondering what to make for dinner.

quick start tip

Let key ingredients do double duty

Save time and money by planning meals that share the same basic ingredients. Examples include bell peppers, chicken, and rice. These items can be used in both Mexican fajitas and Asian stir fry. The following staples are featured in many recipes and should always be found in your kitchen: garlic, onion, olive oil, pasta, rice, canned tomatoes, canned beans, frozen vegetables, and spices.

Become a
Crock pot gourmet

Crock pot cooking is a simple way to feed your family a hot, nutritious dinner. Decide which nights are best-suited for Crock pot dinners. Then, toss meat, vegetables, water, and seasonings into the slow-cooker in the morning, and carry on with your day. By chow time you'll have a nutritious soup, sauce, stew, or hearty dish the whole family will enjoy. Crock pots are especially good for keeping food hot when the family can't eat together.

➔ Use a weekly menu to keep track of calories

Planning menus gives you control over your eating habits. Knowing what you will eat in advance cuts down on grazing and overeating and keeps you healthy without having to diet.

To maximize these benefits, consider calories, fat, fiber, and portion sizes when planning your menus. Do not wait until you are ready to eat to figure out these key components of healthful dining! Put thought into your meals in advance. Doing so increases your ability to make thoughtful choices at the grocery store and in your kitchen.

Cook and freeze
meals for later

Some nights and weekends are so busy that you just won't have time to make dinner. To prevent the fast-food drive-thru from becoming a frequent habit, spend one day each month cooking, storing, and freezing healthy meals. Label freezer bags or containers with the date and enjoy that meal for up to 45 days. With tasty dinners right in the freezer, kids can heat up a portion on their way out the door or your whole family can enjoy a home-cooked meal, no matter how busy your week is.

Coordinate a monthly recipe exchange

Everyone gets tired of their own cooking after awhile. Spice up your culinary repertoire by injecting new life into your menu. Once a month, email 5 of your friends and coworkers one of your favorite recipes, and ask them to do the same. Or, invite a few people over with their favorite dish, along with copies of the recipe.

Try This!

Take-out can be a nice, stress-free option every once in a while. Just don't waste time and energy scrounging for restaurant menus. Set aside space in a drawer for healthy to-go menus from your favorite dining spots, or bookmark their websites in a labeled folder on your online "Favorites" list.

Keep It Organized

NOW

❏ Print your favorite recipes and file them
❏ Purge recipes you know you will never make again
❏ Write recipes on index cards and include nutritional info on the back
❏ Designate one day a week for menu planning

MONTHLY

❏ Get to-go menus from new restaurants in your area
❏ Ask family to review the previous month's menus
❏ Restock cupboards with staple ingredients and spices
❏ Note how much food is wasted or thrown out and make necessary menu changes
❏ Let the kids plan the menu one weekend per month
❏ Leave a few days per month "free" for eating out or bringing home take-out

YEARLY

❏ Purchase a new cooking "toy," such as a wok, Crock pot, or steamer

Moving

Moving is big job made easier by organizing each component—from start to finish. Breaking down relocation into steps is your best hope for avoiding expensive last-minute decisions, and for reducing overall stress.

quick start tip

Create a master to-do list

Write one large list that includes everything involved in your upcoming move. Then, make a second list that breaks down all tasks into 3 categories—Before, During, and After moving day. Organize tasks within the appropriate category in order of importance. Keep it updated and check off items as they are completed.

When in doubt,
get rid of it!

Photographs, family heirlooms, and other sentimental treasures should always be kept. But most of us collect and store useless clutter. Moving is the perfect time to purge your closets and drawers of these items. Have yard sales, sell items online, donate them to charity, and recycle or trash unsalvageable junk. Start this process soon after selecting a moving date.

⊙ Pack at least 2 weeks before you are scheduled to move

Give yourself at least 2 weeks to purge, sort, and pack your belongings—and leave extra time to protect valuables as you pack them.

These 2 weeks should come at the end of an extended move time. If possible, leave at least 8 weeks to plan your move, especially if you are moving long distance. Rushing a move makes an already stressful life change that much more harrowing.

Plan for kids and
pets to be elsewhere

Moving day is stressful for adults. But for young children and pets it can be downright scary. Both kids and pets are used to a dependable routine and steady surroundings, both of which are thrown off-kilter by a move. To calm anxious children and pets, arrange for a family member or neighbor to keep them overnight on the day of the move. Once in your new home, make it your first priority to set up your child's bedroom and the area where pets will spend most of their time.

Hire a professional moving company

Well-meaning friends may offer to help you move, and if cost is a concern, consider this. But a better plan is to hire a moving company to do the heavy lifting. Professional movers are paid to do a job—they won't leave you with a half-unloaded U-Haul. Plus, movers will put your belongings exactly where you want your them, and won't accuse you of being bossy.

Try This!

As you pack, write down items in each box on the box's side. Also, number each box, and write what room it belongs in. Keep a master list of box numbers and contents so you can see if you are missing anything after the move.

Keep It Organized

NOW

- ❏ Choose a moving day
- ❏ Research moving companies and compare prices
- ❏ Compile a list of moving-related tasks
- ❏ Investigate daycare, schools, and employment options in your new area
- ❏ Seek referrals for doctors, dentists, stylists, and other professionals
- ❏ Create a weekly moving calendar of tasks to be completed
- ❏ Set a date for a yard sale

MONTHLY

- ❏ Sell items you won't have room for or no longer need
- ❏ Set aside a portion of your paycheck for moving-related expenses
- ❏ Alert utility companies to your move date to stop service
- ❏ Create a budget based on your new monthly mortgage or rent

YEARLY

- ❏ Insist on spring and fall purges to avoid accumulating clutter

Chores

Between working, raising a family, and making time for hobbies, keeping up with housework is a drag. As a result, chores often fall by the wayside. Creating a chore schedule—and occasionally using a professional housekeeping service—can keep your home clean and organized.

quick start tip

Create a weekly chore chart

Create a weekly chore chart that simultaneously organizes all of the household duties and doles them out to each family member. Include children, giving them easy jobs with clearly articulated steps. Encourage participation with a reward system and make it known that completing chores is everyone's responsibility.

Stock cleaning
supplies

Part of having an organized household means keeping it stocked with the supplies required to run it. Take regular inventory of sponges, rags, paper towels, toilet paper, detergent, and cleaning solutions. Immediately add products to your shopping list once they are used up—and always replenish supplies before the next week of chores.

⟳ Rotate household responsibilities

Avoid falling into chore ruts by rotating who does what in your home. For example, assign laundry and vacuuming to your partner one week while you clean the kitchen and bathrooms—then switch it up the next week. Be mindful of alternating especially crappy jobs—like scrubbing the trash can or cleaning out the refrigerator. Make chore days a little brighter by treating yourselves to take-out and a nice bottle of wine once the house is clean.

Stay on top of
daily messes

One reason chores feel like chores is because most of us let everyday muck and mess build up beyond what is reasonable. Staying on top of daily messes, however, reduces the amount of work required on cleaning day. To maintain order during the week, do the following each day: make your bed, wash and put away dishes, sweep the kitchen floor, pick clothes up off the floor, hang towels up to dry, and put items back where they came from. Cleaning a little every day will keep you from have to clean a lot each week.

Hire a cleaning service once a month

Even with your best cleaning efforts, dust and grime build up over time in sneaky places. To manage behind-the-scenes filth, hire professionals to perform a deep clean once a month. A professionally cleaned house will inspire you to keep up with your chore chart as well as maintain cleanliness in areas you are likely to miss.

Try This!

Nontoxic cleaning solutions protect you from the harsh smell of most commercial cleansers. These products can be toxic to humans, pets, and the environment. Try milder, more pleasant smelling (or unscented) nontoxic cleansers made by companies such as Seventh Generation and Babyganics.

Keep It Organized

NOW

- ❏ Create a chore chart and post it in a prominent location in your home
- ❏ Make a list of cleaning products to purchase
- ❏ Give little kids "mini-chores," such as putting away their toys
- ❏ Buy recycled paper products and use green cleansers
- ❏ Use washable rags to clean surfaces
- ❏ Teach kids to wash their own dishes—or at least to put them in the sink

MONTHLY

- ❏ Change vacuum bags or empty the collection chamber
- ❏ Dust bookshelves, dressers, desks, and other surfaces
- ❏ Recycle old magazines and newspapers
- ❏ Hire a cleaning service to do a deep clean
- ❏ Replace rags, sponges, and rubber gloves

YEARLY

- ❏ Have a garage sale to get rid of unwanted items and create more space

Home

In this
section

Kitchen

The kitchen is the hub of the house. So much activity and traffic can make it hard to keep this critical space organized. When organizing your kitchen, strive for accessibility and order. Items should be easy to reach, simple to take out and put away, and be grouped logically.

quick start tip

Keep countertops clutter-free

No matter the size of your kitchen, it probably feels like there is never enough countertop space. Use under-cabinet storage pieces, such as drawer organizers, to hold utensils. Mount additional organizers under the cabinets, stow toasters and other small appliances when not in use, and keep cookbooks between stylish bookends on top of the freezer instead of on the counter.

Make your kitchen work for you

The kitchen often doubles as a home office and mail center. But keeping unessential items in the kitchen clutters it up. Organize mail, keys, and pens with a hanging mail organizer in the kitchen. Keep countertops and the kitchen table clear of homework and other papers by giving each person in your family a folder in the hanging organizer.

➔ Get rid of items you no longer use

Take everything out of your cabinets and make an honest assessment of what you actually use regularly—then get rid of what needs to go.

For example, there is no reason a family of 4 needs 15 coffee mugs. Keep 8 in circulation and donate the rest or store them in the garage for big parties. Do the same for dishes, glasses, and silverware, and store special occasion dinnerware in another room until it is needed.

Make recycling a no-brainer

Some people are lucky enough to live in a city that divides recycling from trash for them; however, most of us need an organized recycling system that keeps aluminum, paper, and plastic separate from garbage. If you don't have space for several different bins, purchase a special trash can that combines a large compartment for refuse and a smaller one for recyclables. Or, look for stackable bins that slide out, conserve space, and allow you to toss bottles and cans in easily.

Organize tupperware using the Smart Spin Storage System

Food storage containers are great for preserving leftovers, but trying to find the right size top through a sea of plastic can be frustrating. Streamline your cabinets with the Smart Spin Storage System. It comes with 35 to 40 pieces, and all the lids are the same size so they stack easily to save space.

Try This!

Get creative with crates! Wooden fruit crates are the perfect size for storing many kitchen items. They are sturdy, often available for free at grocery stores, and give your kitchen a stylish rustic feel. Crates are especially useful for creating a portable coffee and tea "station" that is practical and unique.

Keep It Organized

NOW
- ❏ Throw away old, clumpy spices and powders
- ❏ Donate extra sets of dishes and unused appliances
- ❏ Remove any items that don't belong in the kitchen
- ❏ Purchase a doggy placemat for under pet bowls
- ❏ Put dishes away immediately after they are dry

MONTHLY
- ❏ Defrost freezer, wash ice trays, and toss old food
- ❏ Check tupperware for cracks, match pieces with lids, and replace as necessary
- ❏ Empty and wipe down cabinets and put everything back neatly
- ❏ Check expiration dates for items stored in the pantry
- ❏ Replenish cleaning supplies and do a deep clean of the kitchen
- ❏ Purge items posted on your refrigerator, such as old appointment cards

YEARLY
- ❏ Evaluate what organizational improvements can be made to your kitchen

Fridge & Freezer

Neglected refrigerators are unappetizing and unsanitary. Take time each week to clean out your fridge. Empty it, throw away expired items, and wash down surfaces with bleach and water solution to kill any bacteria.

quick start tip

Throw away old or expired foods

It is amazing what collects in the back of a fridge and freezer! Check the dates on condiment bottles and trash expired products. Toss items that are frostbitten or that have been in your freezer for more than 45 days. When in doubt of a product's freshness, conduct a "sniff" test. Throw out leftovers more than 3 days old. Wipe down leaky containers and sticky jars.

Have a fridge
blueprint in mind

Groceries and leftovers shouldn't be thrown on any old shelf;
your fridge should be organized to help you find what you
need and eat food before it goes to waste. Keep ready-to-
eat-and-drink items, such as yogurts and leftovers, on the top
shelf so your eye goes right to them when you open the door.
Keep taller items in the back and shorter containers in front,
so nothing is hidden. Keep anything that might leak or drip and
contaminate other foods, such as raw meat, on a bottom shelf.
Store veggies in the crisper drawer, which keeps them fresh.

⊙ Keep condiments upright

Condiments tend to tip over, roll around, and spill every
time you open and close the fridge door. A simple and
inexpensive way to keep bottles sturdy and clean is a
condiment caddy. You can buy a caddy that fits on the
door, or you can make one yourself in minutes! Take a cue
from your neighborhood bar and grill and use an empty
cardboard six-pack holder (cover it in pretty paper, if you
like) to keep your condiment bottles upright.

Date and freeze leftovers

Making a huge pot of pasta sauce is a great way to conserve time, but storing it in the fridge is a waste of space. Break large batches of leftovers down into smaller containers and freeze them. Write the date you made the dish and when it should be thrown out. Most items will lose their flavor after 30 days, so use that as your guideline. Use airtight reusable containers to maintain maximum freshness—and always wait until food has cooled before freezing to keep condensation from turning into frost.

Don't overload your fridge

Storing too many items in your refrigerator clutters the shelves and encourages sloppiness, and not all food needs to go in the fridge, anyway. Apples, bananas, tomatoes, potatoes, onions, peanut butter, avocados, and bread are just a few of the foodstuffs that taste better when stored at room temperature. Get such items into cabinets or decorative produce baskets.

Try This!

The space on top of the fridge can become no-man's-land for clutter. Avoid using it to store fruit or items that will spoil if they are forgotten for a week. Instead, use this space for non-kid-friendly items like liquor, or less-used items like a slow cooker, cookbooks, or a stand mixer.

Keep It Organized

NOW

❏ Throw away old, wilted, leaky, or expired food
❏ Store food back to front according to fresh date and height
❏ Place ready-to-eat items where you will see them first
❏ Wipe down the outside of your refrigerator and freezer
❏ Place photos in magnetized frames and limit how many you hang
❏ Buy or make a condiment caddy for the fridge door
❏ Store butter in a closed container
❏ Plan your meals for the next week to avoid buying extra items

MONTHLY

❏ Deep clean the inside of your fridge
❏ Defrost your freezer
❏ Wash ice trays
❏ Throw away freezer items more than 45 days old

YEARLY

❏ Evaluate whether you should upgrade to a more energy-efficient unit

Hallway Closet

The hallway closet often ends up as the family dumping ground. Items like board games, umbrellas, backpacks, and pet leashes clutter the space and make it impossible to find what you need. Choose a main purpose for your hallway closet, and stick with it.

quick start tip

Empty your closet

Chances are you have no idea what you actually have in the depths of the hall closet. Find out! Empty the closet completely, taking out every last treasure (and horror!) you find. Then, sort each item into one of four piles: Keep, Return to Family Members, Donate, and Toss.

Store soft items
in Space Bags

Space Bags (www.spacebag.com) are excellent organizing tools for homes with limited closet space. They are versatile, easy to use, and can triple your storage space. Place soft items—clothes, coats, blankets, sheets, and towels—inside a Space Bag, zip it shut, and use the hose from your vacuum to suck air from the bag. Once sealed, the bags are airtight and will keep moths and moisture out.

➔ Make the hall closet a "coats-only" space

Designate the hall closet for hanging coats only. Put other articles of clothing in the bedroom closet or in storage.

Think of the hall closet as "high rent" space. Your senior prom dress or old wetsuit can be stored in any other closet in your home. Keep this closet for coats and coats only, and make it a family rule to immediately put other items—such as sports uniforms—in the laundry room or bedroom.

Create more room
with stackable drawers

George Carlin one joked that a house is just a place to keep all your stuff. If you are like most Americans, your stuff is likely to collect in the hall closet at a level that would exceed even Carlin's comedic expectations. To make the most of this space without sacrificing too much stuff, use stackable plastic drawers to store items you are not sure what to do with. Limit their height to one or two drawers to allow hanging items their space.

Make your hallway closet seasonal

Making your hall closet a seasonal space ensures easy access to weather-appropriate gear any time of year. In cold weather, hang up warm coats; store hats, scarves, and gloves in an easily accessible box at the top of the closet. When warmer seasons roll around, store cold-weather items in another room and stock the hall closet with beach towels, light jackets, raincoats, boots, and sunscreen.

Try This!

Use the hallway closet to store grab-n-go items. Think of it as a revolving door—grab what you need on the way out and then put it back on the way in. Anything that doesn't fit this model should be kept in other closets.

Keep It Organized

NOW

❏ Empty your hall closet, sort items, and donate anything you don't need

❏ Designate a spot for shoes, hats, umbrellas, and other items

❏ Screw hooks into the wall inside the closet for hanging pet leashes

MONTHLY

❏ Collect random items in a small laundry basket near the closet and empty it

❏ Remove items from the floor to vacuum or sweep

❏ Reorganize shelves or drawers

❏ Remove articles of clothing you wear infrequently

❏ Make a donations pile

❏ Give prizes to children who hang up their coats regularly

YEARLY

❏ Purchase a few new organizing gadgets, such as storage bins, hanging organizers, and shoe racks

Clothes Closet

The clothes closet often ends up a black hole for orphaned socks, too-small jeans, and half pairs of shoes. Since we only deal with this space when getting dressed or putting away laundry, we rarely take stock of what's inside. Make that your first step toward having an organized clothes closet.

quick start tip

Get real about what you wear

Your closet probably contains your skinny jeans, shirts with the tags still on them, and pieces you haven't worn in months. Be honest with yourself! Get rid of anything that doesn't fit. Pull out items you haven't worn in 6 months or more. Clothing in good condition should be donated or sold. Or set up a fun clothing exchange with your friends.

Store seasonal
clothing out of the way

The most effective use for your clothes closet space is to keep only wearable and high-circulation clothing in it, and store the rest. Purchase Space Bags, plastic bins, and under-bed drawers to stow off-season clothing, such as turtlenecks and winter coats or swimsuits and shorts. Label storage containers according to the season that matches the clothing. Launder or dry clean items before storing them so they are fresh and ready to wear when the right time of year comes around.

➔ Double your hanging space

Most stores that sell housewares carry double bars for inside the closet. This handy tool hooks onto the original bar and hangs down below it.

Closet doublers are inexpensive and a great way to maximize even the smallest closets. In fact, double bars quite literally double your hanging space. An extra bar is especially useful for people with small closets or that have small bedrooms that do not allow for a second dresser.

Store shoes
in style

Finding the right shoe rack—or combination of storage products—depends on the size of your shoe collection, your closet space, and how much room you have to store shoes in other areas of your bedroom. When deciding whether to use shoe boxes, floor racks, compartments, hanging, or over-door organizers, make it your goal to keep your shoes together, in good condition, and easily accessible. Get rid of shoes you rarely or never wear. If shoes appropriate for work are in good condition, donate them to organizations that provide clothes to low-income people looking for jobs.

Get hung up on installing hooks

Hooks are an inexpensive quick fix for bedroom closet clutter. Install over-door hooks to hang heavy items such as purses, robes, pants, and sweatshirts. Use wall-mounted hooks to hang lighter items like nightgowns and belts. Install wall-mounted racks next to your closet for additional options and to encourage hanging clothes instead of throwing them in a pile.

Try This!

Use baskets, bins, and boxes to preserve space. Fold pajamas, linens, and casual clothes and place them inside stylish leather, canvas, or plastic storage boxes. Stack them in the corner of your bedroom to keep clothes off the closet floor. Keep loose items together in woven boxes or baskets lined with cloth.

Keep It Organized

NOW

- ❏ Donate clothes that haven't been worn in 6 months or still have the tags on them
- ❏ Get rid of pieces that don't fit or are outdated
- ❏ Shred stained or torn clothes into strips and use as cleaning rags
- ❏ Organize your closet by activity, such as work, casual, and special occasion
- ❏ Buy fewer cheap or sale items; invest in classic, high-quality pieces that don't lose shape or have to be replaced as often

MONTHLY

- ❏ Hang up any clothes that have fallen on the floor
- ❏ Hang a laundry bag on the back of the door to hold pieces that need to be dry cleaned
- ❏ Vacuum or sweep the closet floor and pick up any loose items

YEARLY

- ❏ Cycle seasonal clothing through your closet
- ❏ Save only one piece of clothing for sentimental reasons

Living Room & Den

The living room is where most families congregate. As a result, coffee and end tables end up cluttered with empty glasses, snack wrappers, and papers. Make it a rule that whatever is brought into the living room must be taken out by the day's end.

quick start tip

Live and let live —within reason

Your ideal living room is likely marred by the reality of sharing space with messy family members. It is vital to your mental health to accept that you cannot control what others do in this shared space. You can, however, lead by example and encourage tidiness by cleaning up after yourself at all times.

Make use of "under" and "in" space

The most common items that cause living room clutter are newspapers, books, magazines, DVDs, CDs, and remote controls. People tend to leave them where they lay and not put them away. Store DVDs in shallow metal bins that slide under the couch; recycle all but the most recent newspapers and magazines, leaving only current issues in a magazine rack; and store remote controls in an end table drawer.

⊖ Get a grip on wires with cable organizers

Most living rooms contain the bulk of a home's electronics. Televisions, DVD players, stereos, speakers, and video game systems can turn a living room into a forest of wires.

To contain your wily wires—and keep children and pets safe—invest in a cable management system. Products such as chord protectors, cable ties, clips and clamps, and wire looms can keep chords safely bound together and out of sight.

Don't
over-decorate

Over-decorating the living room makes it feel more cluttered than it actually is. Knick knacks, picture frames, and wall hangings on every open surface make a room appear small and disorganized.

Fix this by placing just one picture frame on end tables. Remove all but the most significant knick knacks. Keep wall hangings to a minimum. In addition to giving the room a clean feel, removing the majority of these items will open up your living room to shelving and storage options that did not exist before.

Keep coffee and end tables clutter-free

By the end of the day you probably have quite an eclectic collection of items taking up space on coffee and end tables. It is likely some of those items were already there, beneath the new mound of mess. To decrease the amount of time spent cleaning up each evening, keep "base clutter," such as coasters, crossword puzzle books, cups, and games, to a minimum.

Try This!

Assign each family member a basket for their stuff. Keep the baskets stacked in a corner in the living room. And at the end of the day have each person collect their belongings in their basket to take to their own rooms. Use baskets in other areas as well to reduce overall clutter.

Keep It Organized

NOW

❑ Keep your living room well lit
❑ Vacuum (or sweep) at least 3 times per week
❑ Put loose DVDs and CDs back in their cases
❑ Remove half of everything placed on your tables
❑ Get a pet bed and an open bin to store pet toys

MONTHLY

❑ Dust shelves and check wires
❑ Get rid of movies you no longer watch and books you no longer read
❑ Replace batteries in remote controls as needed

YEARLY

❑ Upgrade electronics as necessary
❑ Buy one new piece of furniture that supports your organizing efforts, such as an ottoman with storage space beneath the lid
❑ Sell DVDs, CDs, electronics, and furniture you no longer use

Home Office

The home office is the business center of your house. It is where you do your accounting, pay bills, and keep your most important papers. Keeping it organized is critical to the functioning of your household.

quick start tip

Divide your office into work zones

In addition to your main work center, have a trash, recycling, and shredding corner—preferably near a mail center. Keep paper clips, printer ink, and other supplies in the desk drawer or in a pen cup. Create a scheduling area with a large wall calendar or dry erase board—keep pens, markers, and erasers nearby. Think of your office as having different stations for accomplishing different kinds of work.

Shred, recycle,
and throw it out

Home offices can become graveyards for papers, dried up highlighters, out-of-ink pens, "fix-it" projects, empty ink cartridges, and other deceased office supplies. It is important to purge items that have lost their usefulness! Left to sit, they become deadweight, dragging down your productivity. Clear a path to concentration by getting rid of old or useless office supplies.

⊙ Turn office walls into organizational hot spots

Viewing a poster of a tropical beach may be uplifting, but imagine how great you would feel if that space was transformed into an organizational paradise!

Keep posters, art, and family photos to a minimum in your office. Instead, install shelves, dry erase and cork boards, mail organizers, storage cubbies, and wall-mounted hooks. Use these products to create a superior workspace and save the pretty views for your calendar and screen saver.

Create a mail super center

Mail is difficult to manage because you get more of it every day. Avoid getting buried under the USPS by creating a mail super center in your home office. Make it a point to open and read every piece of mail upon its receipt. Then deal with it immediately. Shred, file, or recycle junk mail. Mount organizers on the wall and group mail into categories. Have a prominent section dedicated to bills that are due within the month. Having a "pay now" section will prevent losing important bills and receiving pink collection envelopes.

Be your own secretary

Become your own secretary and follow the, "Do it now" rule of executing office duties. If you can do it in under 5 minutes, do it now. Some of your immediate duties are to open mail, file documents when you are done with them, put everything back from where it came from, regularly take inventory of office supplies, and keep a clean workspace.

Try This!

Place important office supplies within arm's reach from your chair. Keep a small filing cabinet next to your desk; put your printer on top of the filing cabinet; use the vertical space above your desk to shelve speakers, paper, folders, and books; and set a trash can and shredder within reachable distance.

Keep It Organized

NOW

❑ Clear everything off your desk and wipe it down
❑ Make ergonomic adjustments to your workspace
❑ Only allow one picture frame on your desk—
  hang the rest in the hallway
❑ Sort through office supplies and toss items that do not work
❑ Keep just one notepad on your desk to jot down ideas

MONTHLY

❑ Purge filing cabinets of unnecessary papers
❑ Shred sensitive papers and mail
❑ Empty mail organizers and file paid bills for one month
❑ Reorganize desk drawers

YEARLY

❑ Move important papers into a "long-term" filing cabinet or drawer
❑ Upgrade one piece of office equipment
❑ Store CDs with backed-up files or pictures in a
  CD-organizing book

Bathroom

Almost every guest you have in your home will use your bathroom. Therefore, you should give it the same attention you do your living room or other area you use to entertain. In many ways, your bathroom is a reflection of how you keep you whole house.

quick start tip

Clean bathrooms often

Deep clean bathrooms once a week. Scrub the toilet, shower and sink. Wipe down surfaces and mirrors, and sweep and mop the floor. Wash and replace towels and hand towels, and shake out the bath mat. For daily maintenance, use disinfectant wipes. Keeping bathrooms fresh and clean makes them seem more organized.

Put shelves
in the shower

Shower organizers come in many styles and sizes. Start by assessing your shelving needs. Count how many bottles of shampoo, conditioner, body washes, and soaps you actually need. Next, decide what type of shower organizer meets those needs. Options include shelves installed with a tension rod in the corner of the shower, those that hang from the shower head, and those that attach with suction cups or hardware.

⊙ Make use of the vertical space above the toilet

Maximize bathroom space by installing shelves above your toilet.

There are several units that work for any size bathroom. Measure the space and go from there. Decide in advance what your needs are—do you require a place to store towels, extra toilet paper, or knick knacks? Do you want a free-standing or wall-mounted unit? Your answer will decide the size and durability of your shelving needs.

Hang hooks
and bars

Hooks and bars are an organizing gift for busy families. Over-door hooks work well for hanging heavy robes. Double-row bars are perfect for keeping the bathroom stocked with fresh guest towels. Wall-mounted hooks—placed on walls or at the back of the door—are perfect for hanging wet towels. Make it your goal when implementing these ideas to keep clothes and wet towels off the floor and bed.

Use Caboodles, caddies, and baskets to save your sink

Most bathrooms have limited counter space. As a result, the sink ends up a cluttered mess of toothpaste, hairbrushes, makeup, and contact lens kits. Besides the ick factor of having hair in your toothpaste, this scene is a plain mess. Instead, store like items together in plastic baskets, Caboodles, or caddies under the sink. You still have easy access to your stuff—but it's kept dry, neat, and together.

Try This!

Everyone reads in the bathroom! Acknowledge this universal habit by keeping bathroom reading material fresh and organized in a wall-mounted or free-standing magazine rack. Keep only current issues with short articles to discourage "dawdling" while in the bathroom.

Keep It Organized

NOW

- ❏ Store cleaning supplies in a plastic caddy
- ❏ Keep a container of disinfectant wipes handy for quick a wipe-down
- ❏ Stow the bathroom scale beneath the trash can to conserve floor space
- ❏ Throw away old makeup, deodorants, and any empty bottles
- ❏ Use a net with suction cups to store bath toys
- ❏ Use drawer dividers to organize small items
- ❏ Put a week's worth of cotton swabs in a small container and store the rest

MONTHLY

- ❏ Use heavy-duty mold and soap scum remover in the shower
- ❏ Wash or replace the shower curtain
- ❏ Clear slow drains
- ❏ Restock paper products

YEARLY

- ❏ Replace broken mirrors and faulty hooks, bars, and suction cups

Garage

The garage is usually treated as a catch-all storage space for everything from tools and basketballs to broken lawn mowers and old clothes. Organizing the garage begins with taking stock of what you have, keeping what you need, and selling, donating, or throwing away the rest.

quick start tip

Use color-coordinated storage containers

Make finding things in your garage easier by using color-coordinated storage containers. For example, store holiday gear in red plastic bins; use green crates for garden supplies. Put tools in clear bins with blue tops and use pink crates for party supplies. Then stack all of these containers together to create a mosaic of organization.

Create activity
stations

Most garages are filled with items that fit into one of the
following categories: sports, crafts, lawn and garden, tools,
kid's toys, and memorabilia. To best utilize this space, keep
like items together in designated activity sections. Divide
items into categories and stack them together in different
sections of the garage. Hang a sign above each section that
describes what is contained there.

➲ Build up your storage space

Evaluate your storage needs before settling on a shelving
unit. Shop around to compare prices and types of storage
systems.

Free-standing metal shelves are an inexpensive storage
solution. They are moveable and fairly easy to assemble.
Wall-mounted shelving units are more expensive, but are
sturdier and more permanent. Cabinets are great for storing
weather-sensitive items—and they offer more security
because they can usually be locked.

Put safety before
convenience

The garage can be a dangerous place—especially for kids and pets. As you reorganize this space, make safety your top priority. Chemicals such as antifreeze, oil, lighter fluid, and other hazardous materials should be tightly sealed and stored inside a locked metal cabinet. Put labels on the doors to indicate that toxic items are stored inside. In addition, store all ropes, chords, and wires in sealed containers to prevent falls—and cover sharp corners with padding in case someone does trip.

Get bulky equipment off the floor

Big fun takes up a lot of space! Make room by installing heavy duty hooks and racks to get large, bulky items up off the floor. Surfboards, bicycles, kayaks, soccer nets, fishing poles, and even small boats can be hung from the garage ceiling with the proper hanging system. Consider hiring a professional handyman to ensure the system is installed properly.

Try This!

Print labels for each storage container and list categories for the items in the box. Label boxes, bins, and even shelves according to ownership—"Billy's toys"—or by item and date—"Photographs, 1980-1990."

Keep It Organized

NOW

❏ Pick a day this week to empty and organize the garage
❏ Stock up on plastic storage containers
❏ Decide what your garage is for—storage, studio space, shelter for car, etc.
❏ Use drawer dividers to organize small items
❏ Buy locks for metal cabinets and drawers
❏ Install a smoke detector if you don't already have one

MONTHLY

❏ Put a box in the garage to collect items you plan to donate
❏ Check hazardous materials to make sure none are leaking
❏ Check batteries in garage door openers

YEARLY

❏ Replace batteries in smoke detectors
❏ Have a garage sale
❏ Get rid of 20 percent of the items stored in your garage

Bedroom

When you get dressed for work and before you get ready for bed, make a point to put everything away before moving on to the next thing. Taking a few minutes to do this will keep your bedroom a clutter-free and restful space.

quick start tip

Make your bed every day

Most people say their favorite thing about staying in a nice hotel is walking into a room with a freshly made bed. Give your bedroom this clean, restful feel by making your bed every day. Think of your bed as the room's centerpiece; it should always be in top form. Make your bed each morning, and you'll be surprised how much you enjoy lying down in it each night.

Fold laundry
and put it away

Living out of your laundry basket causes clean and dirty clothes to get mixed up. It also causes clean clothes to wrinkle, making them look dirty all over again. Make it a habit to fold laundry as it comes out of the dryer. Stack folded clothes in piles that go together in drawers, and then put them away. Build in 15 minutes to iron clothes and hang them in your closet.

➔ Keep work out of the bedroom

If your nightstand is piled high with books, files from the office, and magazines, you are working too hard in a space in which you are supposed to be resting.

Your bedroom should be reserved for sleep and sex, and very little else. View your room through the eyes of a sleep expert, and remove anything that looks like work or reminds you of stress. Make your bedroom a sanctuary for relaxation and sleep, and leave your briefcase at the door.

Supplement closet
space with a dresser

Most people have more clothes than space to store them. As a result, clothes end up stuffed into closets, smashed in drawers, or tossed on the floor. Unless your space is truly limited, invest in an additional dresser. The 6 or 8 extra drawers will come in handy for stowing bulky sweaters and sweatpants. Small drawers can be used to house slips, socks, underwear, and other dainty apparel that often gets stuck in the back of overstuffed drawers.

Create a home base for accessories

There are countless products available for organizing your accessories, which means there is no excuse to leave necklaces, earrings, cuff links, and belts lying on top of your dresser. Give these special items a home and you will always know where to find them. Store rings and cuff links in a jewelry box. Hang necklaces from hooks on the wall. Install a belt rack in your closet, and always put items back where you found them!

Try This!

Install track lighting in your bedroom to create atmosphere with light. Wall mounted lights also reduce lamp clutter on nightstands and limit the number of wires running along the floor and behind the bed. Lights designed for above the bed also target your book without keeping your bedmate awake.

Keep It Organized

NOW

- ❏ Purchase drawer organizers and a tray for your phone, watch, and keys
- ❏ Put your bed on risers to create more under-bed storage space
- ❏ Get a bedside organizer to store your book, glasses, and remote controls
- ❏ Hang a mesh bag in your closet for delicate laundry items
- ❏ Put books you are not currently reading back on the bookshelf

MONTHLY

- ❏ Put seasonal clothing in storage
- ❏ Wipe down curtains, blinds, windows, and lamp shades
- ❏ Check behind dressers, nightstands, and under the bed for fallen items
- ❏ Flip your mattress every few months

YEARLY

- ❏ Replace out-of-shape pillows and old sheet sets
- ❏ Paint walls a color that inspires relaxation, such as pale blue
- ❏ Rejuvenate by moving furniture into a new configuration

Child's Room

A child's room is his sanctuary, playground, and one true domain. As such, it is cluttered with toys, art supplies, clothes, stuffed animals, and school books. When organizing your child's room, respect his space and belongings, and include him in the process.

quick start tip

Build the room "up" around an open play space

Kids need an open play area, so get toys, crafts, and books off the floor. Not only does this increase floor space but it also makes the room safer by reducing tripping hazards. Incorporate wall and ceiling storage options in your design, and limit the amount of furniture you add to the room.

Raise the bed
to increase floor space

If your child no longer sleeps in a crib, it is safe to put her bed up on risers. Purchase "drawers" that slide under the bed. Open at the top, these bins make toys, books, and craft supplies easily identifiable—and accessible—to your child. If your child is old enough to climb a ladder, put in a loft bed to increase floor space. Loft beds come in many styles and kids think they are fun!

→ Store it in color-coded bins

What the best children's organization products share is the designer's recognition that kids want "it" now. Whatever it is—crayons, paints, a puzzle, or a ball—your child does not want to search high and low for it.

To meet this need, color-code your child's storage system. Teach your child that puzzles are in red boxes, art supplies are in green bins, and so on. Once your kid knows exactly where "it" is, he is less likely to empty every box and drawer to find what he is looking for.

Use hanging nets
for the soft stuff

Kids like to be able to see their stuff, so hiding toys in a drawer is not their favorite storage system. Toy nets, however, allow kids to keep an eye on their possessions even when they are put away. These handy devices come in several sizes and hang by hooks in the corner. They are great for storing stuffed animals and extra blankets. You can even stack them in one corner of the room and use lower nets to store books or shoes. Small nets are great for closets to hold socks, underwear, pajamas, and diapers. Toy nets are a versatile, inexpensive, and easy-to-install organizational tool for parents and kids.

Double your child's closet space with hanging shelves

Hanging cloth shelves in your child's closet will double storage possibilities. The top of these hanging systems have hooks that fit over the closet bar like hangers. Clothes, sheets, and blankets stay organized without interfering with hanging clothes. Put less-frequently used items higher up, reserving lower space for items that get daily or weekly use.

Try This!

Make it easy for kids to hang up their clothes by putting a step stool in the closet so they can reach the bar—or move the bar down to where they can touch it. Make it a game by timing them to see how many shirts they can hang up in 1 minute and give a reward for each one.

Keep It Organized

NOW

❏ Talk to your child about how to keep his room neat
❏ Invest in a few key items, like a toy chest, hanging nets, or storage bins
❏ Get rid of games and toys that are incomplete or never played with
❏ Make it a rule that your child tidies up his room before going to bed
❏ Start a "Clean Room" reward system

MONTHLY

❏ Vacuum under the bed, behind dressers, and inside the closet
❏ Ask your child to pick one game or toy to give away
❏ Get rid of clothes that are very worn or no longer fit your child
❏ Replenish dried up or empty arts and crafts supplies

YEARLY

❏ Increase your child's organization responsibilities with each birthday
❏ Evaluate whether your growing child needs new age-appropriate furniture

Nursery

You will want to finish preparing the nursery before baby comes home. Allow plenty of time to think about how you want your child's space to look and feel, and make a plan to maximize its level of functionality and convenience.

quick start tip

Reach it with one hand on the changing table

The nursery might be the one room in which you should not put everything away in drawers or the closet. You will want to be able to reach diapers, wipes, tissues, lotions, and creams without stepping away from your baby on the changing table. If you must reach for something, take baby with you and never leave him unattended, even for a minute.

Make the most of
a shared space

Many young families have to set up a nursery in a room that already serves a purpose. If your baby's room will double as the home office, for example, make the most of every inch of space. Build up shelves along the walls, store baby items in a cubby-hole-style wall unit, and keep office supplies together in one area. Keep the functions of these two important spaces as separate as possible. Consider dividing the room with a curtain or large privacy screen.

➔ Don't overstuff the nursery

Fight the urge to fill every inch in the nursery with a decoration or toy. Instead, leave lots of open space for your baby to grow into her room. Indeed, as she gets bigger, so too will her clothes, toys, and need for wiggle room. Unless you have an unusually large nursery, limit furniture to a crib, dresser, small bookshelf, rocker or glider, and a changing table.

Make the nursery
comfortable for you, too

For the first few months of life, the nursery is more for parents than for baby. You will spend countless hours in this room, feeding, singing, rocking, reading to, and watching your baby sleep. Make it a comfortable space that you enjoy spending time in. Hang a clock over the wall to keep track of time. Put up a calendar, and have a pen nearby to write down significant milestones. Place magazines and books that you enjoy in a basket near the rocking chair. Keep your charged iPod with you, and always have a bottle of water and some snacks handy.

Become a basket-case for organization

Exhaustion, a screaming baby, and a dirty diaper make accessibility a priority for nursery set-up. Store diapers, wipes, and other essential baby care products in open bins, baskets, or boxes so that you can quickly find what you need. Cloth-lined baskets are inexpensive and perfect for storing baby's necessities in a stylish way.

Try This!

Your child will be sitting, crawling, pulling himself up, walking, running, tripping, and grabbing everything in sight before you know it. Crawl around on the floor to get a baby's-eye view of areas that need childproofing.

Keep It Organized

NOW

- ❏ Register for baskets and other room organizers before your baby shower
- ❏ Install a few different lighting options in the nursery—low lighting for when baby is sleeping and brighter lights for when you need to see what you are doing
- ❏ Put water and magazines on a small table next to the glider while nursing
- ❏ Decide to use either cloth or disposable diapers—then set up a system that works for quick and easy diaper changes
- ❏ Use a Diaper Genie to store soiled disposable diapers

MONTHLY

- ❏ Hang a bag in the closet to keep too-small clothes you plan to donate
- ❏ Go through toys and get rid of any that have become unsafe or worn out

YEARLY

- ❏ Have a baby-themed yard sale
- ❏ Offer friends with newborns your child's hand-me-downs

Pantry

Your pantry's only function should be to support your culinary efforts in the kitchen. To this end, reserve your pantry for storing food, spices, paper products, and items like Ziploc bags and aluminum foil.

quick start tip

Check, combine, and purge

Rummage through your pantry to check expirations dates. Throw away items past their fresh date as well as half-used packets and hopelessly clumpy powders. Combine any open packages of the same food in clear plastic storage containers. Toss stale chips, crackers, and cereal—and remember to recycle the empty cardboard boxes.

Use wire racks to
increase shelf space

The best way to organize the pantry is to capitalize on its vertical space. Increase your pantry's storage capacity by setting wire racks on the shelves. Wire racks double a shelf's storage possibilities and are a sturdy solution for stacking wobbly cans. Most wire cabinet organizers are adjustable and expandable—up to 43 inches wide! Plus, their open design keeps items visible.

→ Install roll-out drawers

Roll-out drawers are a worthwhile investment for organizing the pantry. Installation is required, but if you own a basic tool set you should be able to do it yourself.

Roll-out drawers and trays come in several shapes and sizes. They can accommodate wine bottles, tall boxes, small appliances, and even trash and recycling receptacles. Drawers generally come with one to three trays that slide easily in and out of the pantry. They make it easy to locate items that would otherwise be shoved in the back of the pantry.

Store dried goods
inside clear containers

Keep your pantry clean and organized by ditching the packaging of foods like pasta, rice, flour, or sugar. Putting dried goods in clear food storage containers keeps shelves free of loose pasta, grains of rice, and granules of sugar. Plastic containers also keep vermin out. Canisters come in all shapes and sizes. Containers usually come in plastic, glass, or acrylic. Some higher-priced containers come with space to write the brand name and purchase date of the item, or you can affix a label to the container yourself.

Clear a path to spices with an over-the-door organizer

An over-the-door organizer is great for keeping spices and seasoning packets visible and accessible. It also opens up high shelf space ideal for keeping vitamins and supplements out of children's reach. Metal over-door racks are attractive and sturdy and range in price from moderate to expensive. A less-expensive alternative is a clear shoe organizer.

Try This!

Most pantry items keep for many months, so stock up on frequently used items when they are on sale. It may feel odd to come home with 6 cans of chickpeas or 10 cans of broth, but after a couple months of chasing sales, your collection will even out and you will always have the ingredients you need on hand.

Keep It Organized

NOW

❏ Group similar products together in the pantry
❏ Remove items that do not belong with food, such as cleaning products
❏ Institute a "finish it before you open a new one" rule
❏ Hang a whiteboard on the outside of the pantry to keep a shopping list
❏ Condense packets—such as oatmeal or Pop-Tarts—into one clear storage container or basket

MONTHLY

❏ Take stock of depleted staples and restock as necessary
❏ Throw away products past their fresh date
❏ Donate one bag of canned food to a local homeless shelter
❏ Stop buying products your family does not finish

YEARLY

❏ Empty the pantry, purge old and half-empty products, wipe down surfaces, and reorganize

Laundry Room

The laundry room is an easy space to organize because its function is limited and obvious. Part of your plan for this room should include encouraging family members to move clothes in and out of this room in a timely manner.

quick start tip

Start a laundry day schedule

If you have a large family, it may seem like someone is always washing something. Help family members keep their clothes separate from each other by assigning each person a unique day on which their laundry may be done (similar to trash day). Plus, assigning each person their own day encourages them to do their laundry on time, lest they have to wait another whole week.

Make the laundry
room sorting central

Purchase a laundry sorter that has 3 compartments—one for darks, one for whites, and the third for delicates. Ask family members to separate items into the sorting bin. Make it a rule that clothes must be sorted, right-side out, and with empty pockets—or else they do not get washed. Have family members leave their personal baskets in the laundry room until their clothes are washed, dried, folded, and ready to be taken to their rooms.

➔ Install shelves above the washer and dryer

The wall space above the washer and dryer is ideal for installing shelves.

Any shelf style will do, but remember that detergents and bleach will likely drip—for this reason, avoid wire rack-type units. Instead, purchase easy-to-clean metal, plastic, or treated wood shelves. Place them high enough so as not to restrict top-loader machines. Store (from left to right) detergent, bleach, stain treatment products, and dryer sheets to increase accessibility.

Create a folding station

Use one wall in your laundry room to create a folding station. The goal is to have a dedicated, clean space to fold clothes as they come out of the dryer. Tabletops should be high enough so you do not strain your back. Purchase a table with shelves below it for additional storage possibilities. Or, for very small spaces, mount a platform that folds against the wall when not in use.

Use a collapsible drying rack for delicates

If you own delicate items that cannot be put in the dryer—such as bras, neckties, and clothes made from special fabrics like silk— purchase a collapsible drying rack. Hang delicate and hand-washable apparel on the rack to dry. Make it a point to remove dried items, collapse the empty rack, and store it until the next round of delicates are washed to keep your laundry room clutter-free.

Try This!

Encourage your kids to do their laundry duty by buying each of them a festive clothes hamper. Choose one with a cartoon or action figure they like, or buy a blank one and let them paint it. Give them a small reward for bringing their dirty clothes to the laundry room when their hamper is full.

Keep It Organized

NOW

❏ Purchase hampers or laundry baskets for each bedroom
❏ Combine half-empty bottles of detergent and recycle empty ones
❏ Wipe down laundry machines and all counter tops
❏ Put a trash can next to the washer/dryer to toss
   pocket trash, lint, and dryer sheets
❏ Hang a cloth bag in the laundry room to collect clothes
   that must be dry cleaned
❏ Install brighter light bulbs

MONTHLY

❏ Scrub laundry room floor
❏ Disinfect washing machine by running a cycle of
   hot water and bleach
❏ Replace chipped or broken laundry baskets and hampers

YEARLY

❏ Move machines to sweep and mop the floor
❏ Consider upgrading to a more energy-efficient washer and dryer

Medicine Cabinet

The medicine cabinet is supposed to be private but many a guest has taken the liberty of peeking. Keep this in mind as you reorganize yours. Ask yourself what the condition of its contents says about you, and whether it's time to craft a new statement.

quick start tip

Make organizing the medicine cabinet part of your cleaning ritual

Because it is small and used often, your medicine cabinet can become quickly disorganized. Stay on top of it by tidying your medicine cabinet whenever you clean the bathroom. It should not take more than a few minutes of weekly maintenance to keep this important area in top shape.

Affix a magnetic
strip to the mirror back

Attach a magnetic strip to the inside of the medicine cabinet and never wonder where your tweezers are again! Magnetic strips are easy to install using self-adhesive on the back of the mirror—or, for more durability, you can screw one directly into the cabinet. Use it to hold small metal objects, such as tweezers, nail files and clippers, lash curlers, scissors, and hairpins.

⊖ Replace packaging with clear storage containers

Having access to pain killers and bandages is sometimes urgent—and you should not have to wrestle with boxes of Q-tips and open bags of cotton balls to get at what you need.

Since a medicine cabinet is a small space designed to hold a few key items, remove boxes, bags, and other bulky packaging that items come in. Then, put items in clear, compact plastic storage containers. Use these to keep a reasonable number of cotton swabs and Band-aids accessible and store the rest under the sink.

Stock the
Big Three

A well-stocked medicine cabinet helps us deal swiftly with minor accidents and ailments at home. Always have a few items within the following Big 3 categories: Over-the-counter pain and cold relievers, first aid supplies, and prescribed medication. Organize your medicine cabinet so that it includes acetaminophen, ibuprofen, cold and cough medicine, a thermometer, bandages, hydrogen peroxide, tweezers, burn and itch creams, and any medications prescribed by your doctor. All other items—such as lotions, makeup, and deodorant—should be secondary to the Big 3.

Toss anything that is old or expired

Some of us are prone to saving half-used lipsticks and old razor blades as if they are some kind of sacred treasure. Don't be afraid to throw out things that are in fact garbage! Get rid of expired medications, old makeup, disabled product dispensers, empty containers, old toothbrushes, broken combs, old lotion samples, and similar items.

Try This!

Store frequently taken medications in a pill tray. Pill trays will help you remember to take your pills and will also keep you from rifling through a whole medicine cabinet of bottles and jars on a daily basis.

Keep It Organized

NOW

❑ Remove items from the medicine cabinet and wipe down shelves
❑ Clean the mirror with streak-free glass cleaner
❑ Use small baskets to store loose items
❑ Organize items by height and keep similar items together
❑ Store one week's worth of cotton products at a time
❑ Install a lock if child safety is a concern
❑ Remove any items guests should not see, like personal medications, condoms, lubricants, etc.

MONTHLY

❑ Replenish Big 3 supplies when necessary
❑ Combine nearly empty products into one container

YEARLY

❑ Consider upgrading to an anti-fog mirror or in-wall cabinet
❑ Check expiration dates on over-the-counter medication and throw away those that have expired

Basement or Attic

Break down the organization of your attic or basement into small, manageable steps. These rooms tend to be home to objects no one knows what to do with; creating order will take time, patience, and a willingness to part with a significant portion of what is stored there.

quick start tip

Mind the clock

Schedule a full weekend—or longer—to organize your basement or attic. If you are the type to become sentimental over pictures, old clothes, and other mementos, set a timer to give yourself no more than a half-hour to go through each box, drawer, or shelf. Otherwise, it will take years to sort through your belongings!

Your trash is
someone else's treasure

Cleaning out your attic or basement will involve throwing out a lot of stuff you just don't have want or need anymore. But someone might. So take a few extra minutes to put things you no longer want into boxes or bags to be donated. For every item you don't want, ask yourself: "Could someone else use this?" If the answer is "yes," donate it to a local organization for the less-fortunate.

⊙ Return other people's belongings to them

Several years' worth of awards, toys, pictures, drawings, clothes, furniture, games, and sports equipment collects in attics and basements. Grown children swear they will come back for their stuff once they are settled. But time passes. Stuff sits. Dust thickens on the shelves, and you are out of storage room.

When reorganizing the attic and basement, make it a goal to reclaim your space. Collect everything that belongs to your kids, cousins, siblings, and friends, and return those goods to their rightful owners.

Moisture-proof
your "keep" pile

Once you donate or sell unused items and return objects to their rightful owners, you are left with a Keep pile. Only the most valued sentimental pieces belong in this group, which likely includes photographs, family heirlooms, meaningful letters, wedding attire, and special childhood mementos. Because these items are so special, they should be protected from temperature changes and moisture damage. Heavy-duty plastic storage containers with lids, airtight Space Bags, and fireproof boxes are great choices for protecting these irreplaceable keepsakes.

Label storage containers and stack according to frequency of use

Label storage containers accurately and include a brief description of their contents. For example: "Holiday decorations: lights, ornaments, and garland." When stacking storage bins, put the most frequently accessed boxes on top. Also, be mindful of where you store breakables, and label oversized or heavy bins to prevent lifting injuries.

Try This!

Preserve old movies and photographs by digitizing them. Transfer old films to DVD. Scan photos to your computer and burn copies of albums onto CDs. Give the original media to grown children or put hard copies into deep storage for future generations to enjoy.

Keep It Organized

NOW

- ❑ Schedule 2 to 4 days for your reorganization project
- ❑ Break tasks down into small steps
- ❑ Make a trip to Goodwill or the Salvation Army to donate items
- ❑ Purchase storage containers, labels, markers, and cleaning supplies
- ❑ Ask your partner and children to make time to help
- ❑ Take measurements for shelves and cabinets you want to install

MONTHLY

- ❑ Inspect the attic and basement for signs of moisture or weather damage, and buy a dehumidifier if necessary
- ❑ Restack seasonal items for easy access
- ❑ Vacuum or sweep the floor

YEARLY

- ❑ Sell, donate, or throw out 20 percent of items in the attic or basement
- ❑ Make necessary repairs to roof, floor, windows, and doors

Work Bench & Tool Shed

Organize your tool shed so it becomes an inviting workspace. Make items easily accessible and give yourself plenty of room to work on projects. A clean and simple design will make you more likely to follow through on home improvement projects.

quick start tip

Take inventory

Pick a warm, sunny day to empty the tool shed. Lay out everything on a tarp so you can see what you have to work with. Wipe down and oil tools that are greasy, dirty, or rusty. Group like items together for when you are ready to put everything away.

Make a blueprint
for your tool shed

Draw the space of your tool shed or work bench on a piece of paper. Write down height and width measurements on your drawing for each side of the room. Make several copies of your "blueprint" to work with and divide the room into sections. Draw as many drafts as it takes until you are satisfied with the configuration and organize tools accordingly.

⊙ Create a work station

Decide whether you want to build or purchase a workbench. If you are handy, consider building it yourself to cut costs. Whether you build or buy, customize the workbench according to your needs.

Stock your work station with basic necessities, such as a drill press, level, wire wheel, electric drill, pliers, hacksaw, sander, vise grips, table saw, Phillip's and flat screwdrivers, hammer, nails, screws, heavy-duty work gloves, and adequate lighting. Then—get to work!

Install shelves, hooks, and brackets

Tool sheds usually have limited floor space, which means you'll probably have to use the walls and ceiling. Working with walls, ceilings, and corners is awkward, but possible. Get some metal shelf units—these are ideal for holding heavy and sharp items, as well as paint and chemicals. When secured against a wall, they are safe, durable, and sturdy. Install brackets, hooks, and magnetic strips above your workbench—and wherever else you need additional storage. Finally, hang hooks from the ceiling to store bulky or oddly shaped items.

Store small items in clear containers

Keep nails, screws and thumbtacks, and other small items in clear containers. Separate and organize them by size, label them, and store them according to frequency of use. Glass mason jars are a good choice because they are inexpensive, thick, and come with secure lids. Higher-end containers sometimes come magnetized to keep small items together.

Try This!

Fill a toolbox with tools you use the most to create a portable work station. Include in your set a hammer, Phillip's and flat screwdrivers, a variety of nails and screws, a flashlight, work gloves, and an assortment of wrenches. Take it with you in the car or store it in the house for simple repairs.

Keep It Organized

NOW

- ❏ Measure the available space in your shed
- ❏ Establish a reorganization budget
- ❏ Decide whether to build or buy a workbench, or upgrade your current one
- ❏ Purchase shelves, hooks, brackets, storage containers, and other gadgets
- ❏ Start a home improvement library
- ❏ Dedicate one section of your tool shed to lawn and garden equipment

MONTHLY

- ❏ Clean the tools you use the most
- ❏ Sweep the floor and check for items that have fallen
- ❏ Perform general maintenance on power tools
- ❏ Restock nails, pencils, and other items

YEARLY

- ❏ Donate, sell, or throw away tools you no longer use
- ❏ Get a subscription to a favorite home improvement magazine

Important Documents

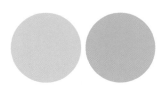

In this section

Correspondence

Email, phone calls, text messages, snail mail ... people have more ways than ever to get in touch with one another, which is overwhelming. Organizing the hefty build-up of daily correspondence starts by saving only the most significant sentiments.

quick start tip

Keep in touch

Schedule a date once a month to connect with loved ones and old friends. Leave a voicemail to say, "I'm thinking of you," then a send short note with a recent photo of your family. Send an email that is at least a few paragraphs long to someone you haven't connected with in awhile. Small gestures like these go a long way in preserving even the most sporadic and long-distance relationships.

Create a correspondence kit

Make getting in touch easy and creative by building yourself a correspondence kit. Keep your address book, pens, stationary, cards, and stamps together and neatly organized in a lunch box, pretty tin, or decorated shoe box. Personalize your letters with monogrammed paper and envelopes that have your return address printed on them. These supplies make it more inviting for you to craft letters and cards.

→ Stock cards for any occasion

Even though birthdays, holidays, and special moments occur all year round, people are rarely prepared in advance for them. This phenomenon keeps the "belated" line of greeting cards in business! Cut down on the number of belated cards you send by keeping a healthy stock of birthday, thank you, sympathy, and blank all-occasion cards on-hand. These will help you be ready to send the right card at the right time.

Give thanks
within 7 days

There are certain occasions for which thank you cards are always necessary. They include receiving wedding, shower, or hospital stay gifts; having a party thrown in your honor; receiving a gift in the mail; and after having been a house guest. Make it your personal policy to send thank you cards within 7 days of any of these events. You can also send friends and family thank you cards any time you feel moved to express your gratitude for their contributions to your life.

File letters and cards after reading

Make it a point to file letters and cards immediately after opening them. Create a filing system that works for you. If you correspond with the same few people, title folders with their names for their letters and cards. Or, organize your correspondence by date or occasion. File only letters and cards that hold sentimental value, or you will quickly run out of room in your filing cabinet.

Try This!

There are some sentiments that are so thoughtful that you want to read them over and over. Put your most meaningful letters together in one scrapbook that you can flip through often. Fill it with cards and letters that deserve to be liberated from the depths of a filing cabinet.

Keep It Organized

NOW

❑ Frame diplomas, letters of acceptance, and award certificates
❑ Create a filing system that works for your correspondence style
❑ Stock up on special occasion and blank greeting cards
❑ Store love letters and other meaningful letters in a decorated box
❑ Write a letter to someone you haven't seen in awhile
❑ Leave notes in your kids' lunch boxes
❑ Create folders in your email to sort e-correspondence

MONTHLY

❑ File meaningful letters and cards
❑ Shred or throw away letters you do not want to keep
❑ Keep up with thank you cards
❑ Restock your correspondence kit

YEARLY

❑ Purge letters and cards that you no longer want to keep

Magazines, Mail & More

Some days you need a wheelbarrow just to cart in all the mail, newspapers, magazines, and catalogs that are delivered to your home. Cut down on what comes in by opting out. Start by removing your address from the Direct Marketing Association mailing list at www.dmachoice.org.

quick start tip

Divide and conquer

As soon as you bring in the mail, divide it into multiple piles—bills, important documents, personal letters and cards, and junk. Stack magazines, newspapers, and catalogs in another pile to peruse at your leisure. Immediately toss junk mail into the recycle bin. Set bills and important documents near your desk and don't open them until you can give them your full attention.

Dedicate just one
place for mail

Create a mail center in your home office or kitchen. Always deal with your mail in this area soon after it arrives. Stock your mail center with wall-mounted wire racks, a shredder, and a trash can. Keep clearly marked folders handy to organize bills, letters, invitations, and other mail. Make it a rule that once a letter is opened, it must move on to the next stage in your mail processing system quickly. Make a pledge to pay, RSVP, file, toss, or otherwise respond to each piece of mail within 48 hours.

⊃ Recycle newspapers after reading

Newspapers end up collecting in the strangest places in peoples' homes—under the dining room table, in the bathroom, and even behind dressers. If you tend to cart your daily paper around the house, do a sweep of all your rooms. Collect old newspapers and throw them in the recycle bin or bundle them for recycling pick-up. For day-to-day organizing, keep a newspaper basket in the room where you do most of your reading, and clean it out twice a month.

Update your
magazine rack

Magazines are written to capture current events. But some people have issues in their magazine racks that are more than 6 months old! Keep only the latest issues of your favorite mags in strategically placed locations throughout your home. Storing magazines in a few different places makes them accessible and prevents one rack from becoming overstuffed. Also, storing magazines in wall-mounted and floor racks instead of in stacks keeps the covers neat and prevents subscription cards from slipping out and littering your floor.

Get crafty with catalogs

Whether you asked for them or not, catalogs somehow find their way into your home. You can recycle these, or get creative with them—use pages to wrap gifts, to decoupage a new journal, or to protect tabletops when you do crafts with your kids. Think of catalogs as decorative scrap paper that you have many uses for.

Try This!

Many companies sell your information to marketing agencies when you order a catalog or shop online. Opting out of this system, the Abacus database, can stave off even more junk mail. Contact Epsilon Data Services, P.O. Box 1478, Broomfield, CO 80038 and tell them to remove your name from their list.

Keep It Organized

NOW

❏ Call 1-888-5-OPT-OUT to reduce the amount of credit card offers you get

❏ Opt out of real estate solicitations by contacting Innovis Consumer Assistance at P.O. Box 1358, Columbus, OH 43216-1358

❏ Contact Equifax Direct Marketing Solutions at P.O. Box 740241, Atlanta, GA 30374 to be removed from their direct marketing mailing list

❏ Contact Christopher L. Irving, Sr., Director Consumer and Privacy Affairs at the Publishers Clearinghouse, 382 Channel Drive, Port Washington, NY 11050 to stop receiving sweepstakes offers

❏ Visit www.nocards.org to learn how your privacy is compromised when you sign up for rewards cards with your supermarket

MONTHLY

❏ File magazines and newspapers that mark significant world, historical, or sporting events

YEARLY

❏ Start your "opt out" campaign over if necessary

Email

Between work, personal, and solicitation messages, the average American receives between 20 and 50 emails each day. This means your inbox sees more than 15,000 new emails per year! Organizing 15,000 of anything is a challenge, but one that can be met with a solid organizational system.

quick start tip

Leave messages marked as unread

Most of us read email the second it comes in. In fact, new mail has a Pavlovian effect on many of us! But reading an email before you are ready to write back causes it to drown in a sea of unhighlighted messages. Therefore, leave emails marked as unread until you are ready to respond. If you can't resist, mark a message as unread after you have read it to remind yourself to go back to it.

Use descriptive
words in the subject line

Always include a word or phrase in the subject line that captures the essence of your message. It helps the receiver know immediately what you're writing about and also where or how to file it. Descriptive subject lines also make the search function work better when you're trying to find a specific e-conversation down the road. Avoid cleverly worded or cryptic subject lines that you won't remember later. "Michael's guitar lesson" will come to your head when searching for an email more than the subject line "My little music man" will.

→ Limit e-subscriptions

Subscribing to websites and blogs you like is a great way to make interesting content find you. But RSS feeds, online news updates, and daily horoscopes will fill your inbox faster than you can say, "I love your blog!" So limit your online subscriptions to 5 or less and visit other websites only when you are moved to read them.

Create e-folders
for filing emails

Online folders are an effective way to organize emails and most programs allow you to create an unlimited number of them. Consider the following when designating folders for your emails: How do you want information grouped? Do you repeatedly get emails that fall into certain categories? What is the best way to search through folders to find a specific message?

Use organizing software

If you receive hundreds of emails a day, get help from filing assistant programs such as SpeedFiler and MsgFiler, which organize your messages automatically. Next-level organizing software such as Nelson Email Organizer or Omea Pro sort email according to information in the messages, such as the date, name of sender, subject line, and keywords. They also set up a searchable index for you.

Try This!

Open a free webmail email account just for junk mail. Nowadays it is common for people to supply an email address when they enter a contest or access a website. Much like a fake phone number, use your junk mail email address to protect your real one from unwanted spam.

Keep It Organized

NOW

❏ Delete emails you no longer need and print and file meaningful ones
❏ Create an online filing system that works for your e-style
❏ Research organizational software options
❏ Set up a spam folder to collect junk mail
❏ Set up separate work and personal email accounts
❏ Ask people who write to you to always include a detailed subject
❏ Delete sent emails that you no longer need
❏ Unsubscribe from all but 5 mailing lists

MONTHLY

❏ Update your security settings
❏ Update your address book

YEARLY

❏ Open a new email account if your old one has been compromised by too much junk mail

Important Papers

Most of us don't realize how much of our lives exist on paper—until we desperately need a piece of information we can't find. Make sure all your important documents are both tightly secure and easily accessible when you need them.

quick start tip

Fill gaps in your paperwork

Gather all of your important documents and spread them out on the dining room table. Make a checklist of what you should have, and compare it to the documents on your table. Highlight those that are missing—an original copy of your birth certificate, for example, or your social security card—and work on acquiring them.

Store important
papers in a secure box

Store all your important documents in a fire and waterproof box, or in a file cabinet that locks. If you are concerned about storing sensitive documents, such as stock and bond certificates or adoption papers, in your home, rent a safety deposit box at your bank. Additional documents to include in a protective lockbox include marriage and death certificates, wills, life insurance policies, titles, deeds, passports, social security cards, naturalization papers, and birth certificates.

→ Create a travel health file

No one wants to think of what can go wrong on a trip. But the reality is there is always a risk of injury or illness when you are on vacation. Carrying a "just in case" travel health file is one way to expedite treatment in the event of an emergency. Include copies of your insurance card, a list of health problems, copies of your prescriptions, any known allergies, and a copy of your immunization records. The extra-cautious can have these documents translated into the language of the country to which they are traveling.

Make copies of
important documents

Some documents are so sensitive, copies will not suffice when you need to present them. However, you may need information from these documents frequently, and thus may not know whether to keep them on hand or in a secure place. A good way to deal with this is to keep a copy of these documents at home and originals in a rented safety deposit box at your bank. An example would be your child's social security card. You may need the number frequently, but you rarely need the card. Protect the original by keeping it at your bank.

Tell someone you trust where to find important documents

After your documents are filed, choose a trusted next-of-kin or extremely close friend to tell where your wills, deeds to burial spots, birth certificates, custody agreements, insurance policies, and other important documents are. In the event you are suddenly incapacitated, you will need someone to get these for you.

Try This!

Photocopy the contents of your wallet. It is likely your wallet holds social security numbers, credit cards, your driver's license, store credit receipts, and more. In the event your car, purse, or wallet is stolen, you will know exactly what you are missing.

Keep It Organized

NOW

❑ Gather all your important documents and make a list of ones you need

❑ Scan your passport, driver's license, and a credit card to store on your computer in case you ever need someone to email them to you while traveling

❑ Protect sensitive information in a rented safety deposit box

❑ Create files for finances, taxes, health, home, auto, children, and travel

❑ Shred documents with outdated contact information

❑ Start working on your will if you do not already have one

MONTHLY

❑ File tax-significant receipts, bills, and invoices

❑ Update emergency contact information and post on your freezer

YEARLY

❑ Notify your insurance company of any major life changes

❑ Purge your files of any documents that are no longer important to you

Finances

A 2007 study by Princeton Survey Research Associates International found that 20 percent of Americans do not pay any attention to their finances. As a result, people incur high interest rates, overdraft charges, debt accumulation, and more. Tracking your finances puts you in control of your financial future.

quick start tip

Track your cash flow

Follow your money's ebb and flow by setting up a tracking system. Write down every dime that comes in and every penny that goes out. Use a notebook and pencil, an Excel spreadsheet, or purchase money organizing software. Include income from jobs and investments and deduct from the total whenever you make a purchase. This way, you won't be left wondering where your income went at the end of the month.

Go
paperless

All of the paper that bills, credit card offers, and bank statements are printed on gets overwhelming fast. Important financial information often gets buried in piles never to be seen again. Going paperless will cut down on this problem and will also get you to centralize your finances on your computer. Ask credit card companies and banks to email your statements and sign up for direct deposit and withdrawal programs. Use Excel spreadsheets or software like Quicken to keep track of your finances.

⊙ Turn part of your home into a financial center

Carve out space in your home for keeping track of your money. Stock your financial center with tools that help you crunch the numbers. Have handy a calculator, pencils, a filing cabinet, several folders, labels, a shredder, a trash can, and whatever you use to manage finances—a notebook or computer, for example. If you and a partner do bills together, keep conversations about finances limited to this area, too.

Divide up your money pie

Represent your monthly income as a pie with slices— these slices represent money you allocate to various expenses. Your money pie must be cut into enough slices to feed your rent or mortgage, utilities, credit cards, grocery bills, savings accounts, household expenses, student loans, and entertainment needs. If your expenses take up too many slices of pie, this visual will immediately reveal problem areas that require further analysis. The pie will also reveal whether you are spending too much on any one slice.

Categorize your purchases for one whole month

People who don't categorize their purchases usually spend more than what they want to spend on discretionary items without even realizing it! Categorize your expenses, evaluate your areas of spending at the end of the month, and you will have a clearer picture of where to cut back. You might learn you can skip a few Starbucks runs or eat out less.

Try This!

Each time you get paid, put money in clearly marked envelopes for grocery shopping, dining out, household needs, and entertainment—and do not spend more than what's inside the envelope. If you can stick to this cash budget, you can avoid accumulating interest on credit cards.

Keep It Organized

NOW

- ❏ Start collecting receipts
- ❏ Establish a realistic budget
- ❏ Open a savings account and retirement account
- ❏ Write down fixed expenses such as rent/mortgage, insurance, and loans
- ❏ Make a plan for reducing flexible expenses, such as dining out
- ❏ Limit financial calculations and discussions to one area of the house

MONTHLY

- ❏ File currently paid bills and receipts
- ❏ Shred unnecessary receipts
- ❏ Tweak your budget and adjust spending as necessary
- ❏ Chip away at credit card debt
- ❏ Keep track of receipts for potential tax deductions

YEARLY

- ❏ Consider a big change—such as a move—to reflect your financial reality

Receipts

When it comes to collecting receipts, most people either go overboard, keeping every receipt ever issued—or they throw them out immediately, only to regret it later. Organizing your receipts will be snap once you have a system for evaluating which receipts are worth keeping and which are not.

quick start tip

Choose when you get a receipt

If you are trying to establish a monthly budget, you'll want to get a receipt for everything you purchase. But if you already have a budget, it makes sense to minimize which receipts you keep. Always keep receipts for big-ticket items, items that are tax-deductible, or ones you suspect you'll return. For small purchases, like coffee or a sandwich, tell the cashier you don't need a receipt.

Start a "30-day"
receipt folder

Keep track of recent purchases by making a "30-day" receipt collection envelope. Punch a hole in a large manila envelope and hang it from a cork board in your home office or insert it in your daily planner. Easy access makes stashing receipts for clothes, gifts, and food a breeze. At the end of each month sort through the receipts, throw out any you don't need, and file the rest.

⊃ Create an e-filing cabinet for online receipts

Shopping online is a great way to compare costs and get the best deal without having to ever leave your chair. But even though you bought online, your purchase comes with records that must be organized.

You can either print a copy of your online receipts and file it with your other receipts, or create an "e-filing cabinet." Create folders in your email or on your desktop in which to store e-receipts. Name folders by purchase month and create subcategories based on types of products.

Treat receipts
as records

Receipts are your proof that you paid money for a product, donated something to charity, and deposited or withdrew money from the bank. They are important records for balancing your checkbook, filing your taxes, and for evaluating how closely you are sticking to your budget. Therefore, you should treat them like important records, because they are. Thinking about your receipts as important documents will help you give them the attention and priority they deserve.

Protect "big" receipts from theft or loss

"Big" receipts such as deeds, titles, and insurance policies should be kept in locked or secure boxes. Store these important records in the same place after each use so that you have immediate access to them. Another option is to keep copies at the house and store the originals in a safety deposit box at your bank.

Try This!

Save your receipts in an accordion folder that has multiple tabs. Tab categories can include "meals," "house supplies," "groceries," "entertainment," "vendor invoices," "automotive," "for the kids," "prescriptions," and others.

Keep It Organized

NOW

- ❑ Sort receipts into categories
- ❑ Shred ATM records that are more than 30 days old
- ❑ Devote one hanging folder in your filing cabinet to receipts
- ❑ Staple receipts to warranties and note the expiration dates on your calendar
- ❑ Remember to give gift receipts with presents
- ❑ Ask for a receipt after making donations
- ❑ Tape receipts to items you plan to return

MONTHLY

- ❑ Compare receipts with bank statements
- ❑ Use the previous month's receipts to shape this month's budget
- ❑ Keep business-related receipts in your tax file

YEARLY

- ❑ Purge filing cabinet of old or unnecessary receipts

Taxes

Tax season can sneak up on people who are disorganized. Take charge of your tax situation beginning in February, and keep up with it year round to minimize the last-minute stress of hunting down documents, receipts, and paperwork.

quick start tip

Create a tax prep checklist

Ease your way into tax season by using a checklist to guide you toward collecting the documents you need well before you need them. Create your own based on your previous filings or print the list provided by TurboTax on their website: http://turbotax.intuit.com/tax-tools. Either way, know what you need long before the April 15th deadline.

File as
you go

Keeping up with your tax situation year round will reduce stress overload in April. First, dedicate an entire drawer in your filing cabinet to tax documents. Stock the drawer with several hanging and manila folders. Organize folders by categories and keep them current by year. Examples include income, donations, home business, interest paid on student loans, investments, bank records, and medical expenses. Everything will be at your fingertips when it comes time to do your taxes.

➔ Use money-organizing software

Programs such as Quicken and Microsoft Money allow you to keep track of your finances, create budgets, and then export all of this information into tax preparation software. They also seek out hidden deductions that may not be obvious to you. These products vary in cost and levels of service, so do your homework before purchasing a package.

Keep receipts that
support deductions

The government allows taxpayers to take many kinds of deductions. Homeowners, those who pay for childcare, and the self-employed should all keep receipts and other documentation to back up any claimed deductions. If you are unsure if you are allowed to deduct it, keep the receipt anyway, just in case. Sort receipts, utility bills, invoices, and other relevant documents into separate folders to keep documents neat and organized. Keep these receipts for at least 3 years after you file your taxes, as you will need them if you are ever audited.

Start early in the year and anticipate what is coming

The sooner you put your tax file together, the less work you have to do in April. Begin your tax preparation in January. Anticipate information that will be issued on W-2s and 1099s and estimate your tax bill. Anticipating what's coming also helps you quickly identify any mistakes made on the tax documents that are sent to you.

Try This!

Do your own taxes! Too often, people pay others to do their taxes because they are afraid they will mess them up. But Turbo Tax, H&R Block, and other tax preparation software programs make filing your taxes very simple and accurate. Doing your own taxes is empowering and easy with the right software.

Keep It Organized

NOW

- ❏ Find a home for your tax file
- ❏ Collect receipts and canceled checks for child care
- ❏ File receipts for paid college tuition
- ❏ Monitor investment income and losses
- ❏ Choose a system to track your finances, like Quicken or Microsoft Money
- ❏ Create a tax prep checklist

MONTHLY

- ❏ File receipts that support your deductions
- ❏ Put money away quarterly to pay taxes if you expect to owe
- ❏ File interest statements from your student loan payments
- ❏ File interest and dividend statements from your investments

YEARLY

- ❏ File W-2s and 1099s
- ❏ Make an appointment with a CPA or purchase tax preparation software

Possessions

In this
section

Computer

Your computer is probably at the center of all of your work and personal business. Therefore, it is important to keep it as clean and organized as you would your desk, office, or other kind of workspace.

quick start tip

Create an ergonomic workspace

An ergonomically designed workspace is one that takes the size and shape of your body into account, maximizing your comfort while sitting for long periods of time. An ergonomic workspace means that the placement of your monitor, chair, mouse, and desk minimizes repetitive stress injuries on your back and joints. An ergonomic workspace will help you work more efficiently and get more done.

Go
wireless

Wires clutter your desk and take up valuable workspace. In this day and age, there is no reason for such a mess. For very little money you can build an impressive and totally wireless work station. Switch out your bulky wired gadgets for a wireless mouse, keyboard, and printer. Also, call your cable company to get outfitted for wireless internet.

⊙ Clean up your desktop

Does it take you 5 minutes to find a file on your computer's desktop? If so, you have too many icons and documents stored there.

Computers come with clean-up wizards that will walk you through organizing your desktop. The program will remove rarely used files and store them in your computer's archives. It will also get rid of unused and duplicate shortcuts. You can even set the clean-up wizard to scan and organize your desktop every 30 or 60 days. Keep your desktop organized by creating folders and storing documents and pictures in them.

Back up
your files

Backing up your files is the single most important thing you can do with your computer. You should buy an inexpensive memory stick—a small, portable device that stores up to 32 GB worth of documents, music, and picture files. Another option is to back up files online, using free programs like Google Docs. Finally, you can invest in a portable storage device that lets you back up the contents of your entire hard drive.

Use an all-in-one printer

Save time and money by buying an all-in-one printer. Companies like Canon, Brother, and HP have printers that combine all your printing needs. With one affordable machine you can print black-and-white or color documents, make copies, print high-quality photos, send faxes, and scan just about anything—in just a fraction of the time it would take to go to Kinko's.

Try This!

Buy an external hard drive. External hard drives are an excellent solution for people who store lots of photos and music on their computers. External hard drives dramatically increase your storage space—up to 500 GB! They come in floor, desktop, and portable models to fit any workspace and budget.

Keep It Organized

NOW

❑ Clean your computer monitor
❑ Run your desktop clean-up wizard
❑ Delete files you no longer need and back up everything else
❑ Protect your computer from viruses by purchasing security software
❑ Protect your bandwidth by setting a password for your wireless internet
❑ Check for software updates and install them

MONTHLY

❑ Delete cookies
❑ Organize your bookmarks or favorites tab
❑ Archive old files

YEARLY

❑ Move all new files to an external hard drive or memory stick
❑ Hire a professional, such as the Geek Squad, to maintain your computer
❑ Get the latest operating system available for your computer

Jewelry & Accessories

Jewelry and accessories are fun to shop for, but once brought home, many rarely get worn. Make it your goal to have easy access to frequently used pieces and commit to wearing other pieces more regularly.

quick start tip

Assess what you have

It is likely that your dresser is full of accessories from years—even whole eras—past. Lay out belts, scarves, and ties on the bed, then sort them into Keep, Donate, and Toss piles. Do the same for your jewelry, adding a Fix It pile for pieces that need to be repaired. Throw out earrings that have lost their mate and give away scarves that make you roll your eyes and say, "What was I thinking?!"

Install a wall-mounted jewelry closet

Wall-mounted jewelry closets are a good option for people with an extensive collection. These decorative storage pieces come small or large to fit just about any space. Large models can hold more than 36 necklaces, 20 rings, and 72 pairs of earrings. As an added bonus, the outside of the cabinet is a full-length mirror, and the door can be outfitted with a key or magnetic lock.

➔ Utilize a ring dish and necklace tree

Necklaces become tangled and knotted and earrings often lose their mates. Try hanging them on a necklace tree—a wire or metal stand with separate branches from which to hang necklaces and earrings with hooks.

You should also make use of a ring dish, which helps keep rings in one spot. You can make your own out of a small bowl, sauce dish, or even an empty seashell. Or, if you buy one, look for a dish with a finger-shaped ring holder in the center, which lets you stack your rings.

Buy several
accessory hangers

Hang ties, belts, and scarves to keep them neat and visible to you. Traditional hangers are acceptable, but a better solution is to use an accessory hanger. This inexpensive wire organizer hangs from your closet rod or hook. It comes in different sizes and has separate sections for different items. Since they are so affordable—about $4.99 apiece—stock up on a few, dedicating one to scarves, one to ties, and one to belts.

Keep a valet tray on your nightstand

Valet trays are a storage option for items that get daily use. Made of leather and lined with felt or satin, these decorative organizers preserve the condition of your most valuable pieces. Keep one on your nightstand to hold your watch, bracelets, rings, cuff links, and cell phone. Make it a habit to leave those items in the same spot every night so you know exactly where everything is.

Try This!

The next time someone asks what you want for a gift, say a jewelry box. Compartments in different shapes and lengths make for easy access. Besides, jewelry boxes make sentimental gifts when engraved with a heartfelt personalized message.

Keep It Organized

NOW

❑ Make Keep, Donate, Toss, and Fix It piles for all jewelry and accessories
❑ Clean your jewelry using cleaner or soap, water, and a soft toothbrush
❑ Buy a necklace tree and ring dish, or make your own
❑ Take broken jewelry or watches with dead batteries in for repairs
❑ Purchase a portable jewelry organizer for when you are on-the-go
❑ Hang ties on multi-layered hangers
❑ Insure your most expensive pieces of jewelry

MONTHLY

❑ Store cold-weather scarves, hats, and gloves in bins until you need them
❑ Save up for an armoire or wall-mounted jewelry closet
❑ Commit to wearing an accessory you haven't worn in awhile
❑ Check behind dressers for fallen accessories

YEARLY

❑ Have wedding and engagement rings professionally cleaned

Books

Turn the chore of organizing your books into a labor of love. Pore over your favorite excerpts and re-read inscriptions. Reminisce about reading the right book at the perfect time, and remember how certain stories helped shaped the person you've become.

quick start tip

Thin out your collection

Books are like old friends and are difficult to part with. But it's likely you have several in your collection you no longer need. Donate or sell books you know you will not read again. Get rid of torn or warped books and old textbooks that sit around collecting dust. And don't worry, you can always track down a title again if you find you miss it and want it back.

Arrange books
by subject and size

You don't have to use the Dewey decimal system to have an organized personal library. A simple way to impose order is to group books by category: fiction, mystery, how-to, self-help, fantasy, and nonfiction are a few types you might have in your collection. Then, arrange those categories by height. Set your nicest books on eye-level shelves. Stacks can be arranged both vertically and horizontally to create an appealing aesthetic.

⊙ Alphabetize books by author's last name

A slightly more time-consuming, yet comprehensive way to organize your books is by author's last name.

Gather your books and put them in piles from A to Z according to author name. Once all books are laid out by letter, go through each pile and alphabetize them by specific author name. Leave a little space on the shelf for future additions.

Try book-swapping
websites

Many books, like novels, are perfect for reading once and passing on. Book-swapping sites like PaperbackSwap.com allow you to unload your clutter by trading used hardbacks, paperbacks, and even audiobook titles for new ones. You simply create a list of the books you want to lend to other members and request the books you want to borrow. When you're done with a book, you mail it back! Book-swapping keeps books you won't reread from piling up on shelves and end tables.

Get creative with your stacks

How you organize your books is a personal choice. It should reflect your style, personality, and make it easy for you to find a specific title. Get creative! Organize your books according to size or color; stack books on the floor to look like a cityscape; store cookbooks in hanging baskets in the kitchen; and keep a collection of short stories in a magazine rack in the bathroom.

Try This!

Arrange books artfully with stylish bookends. Check thrift stores for inexpensive, unique pieces that are heavy enough to hold back books. Use an antique bowl or mixer to display vintage cookbooks and add flair to your kitchen, for example. Other items to look for: vases, clocks, pretty boxes, or figurines.

Keep It Organized

NOW

- ❏ Dust and empty your bookshelves and decide which books to keep
- ❏ Stop buying books until you organize the ones you have
- ❏ Sell old textbooks
- ❏ Set up a book exchange with your friends
- ❏ Start an online book exchange to trade with others
- ❏ Sign up for a library card

MONTHLY

- ❏ Check the condition of your books in storage
- ❏ Allow your child to buy a new book
- ❏ Read one book from your shelf
- ❏ Give old books as gifts

YEARLY

- ❏ Take stock of what books you want to keep and sell or donate the rest
- ❏ Make a substantial book donation to your local library

Music Collection

Music technology is constantly evolving. As a result, you likely have a mix of vinyl, cassettes, CDs, and digital music files. Music spread across so many sources can become wildly disorganized.

quick start tip

Get rid of redundancies

With so many ways to own music, it is likely you own the same album or song in several different forms. Perhaps you have an old cassette that you bought on CD, which you then made a copy of to keep in your car, and then loaded into your computer when you bought an iPod. You only need an album in one or two places, so go through your collection and weed out duplicates.

Give your CD
collection a good home

Not everyone is ready to stash their CDs and go totally digital. To display your CD collection, install wall-mounted media shelves. Or, go with a tall, skinny bookshelf that fits in the small, unused spaces between doorways and in corners. Finally, consider stowing your CD collection in the drawers of a chest or cabinet, which lets you use the top for a stereo, speakers, or vase.

→ Put CDs in book organizers

Move your CD collection into books. These are portable and take up very little space. Store CD inserts with the discs and throw away or recycle the plastic jewel cases, which get dusty and look sloppy.

Organize your CDs alphabetically by artist or band name, and label the outside of each book to indicate the range of letters inside. Get colorful, cloth-covered three-ring binders to make adding pages easy and displaying them attractive.

Purchase software
to organize e-music

The average collector has thousands of music files on his computer. But many of these downloaded files have no information attached to them, which makes them impossible to find. Music organizing software can help get your digital music under control. Programs can also impose order on uploaded CDs. Such software can make your music collection searchable by cover art, artist names, track listings, length of songs, genre, record label, or release date, and more.

Create playlists for your portable music players

Portable music players—iPhones, iPods, the Microsoft Zune, or other kinds of MP3 players—are increasingly popular devices, but the digital music they hold can get out of control fast. Keep your MP3 player organized by creating and naming playlists as soon as you upload music. Combine albums by the same artist, and don't keep your whole collection on your player.

Try This!

Save space and preserve your vinyl recordings by digitizing them. Purchase (or rent) a specialized record player that converts vinyl recordings into digital files. Some plug directly into your computer. Once digitized, sell your records or put them in deep storage.

Keep It Organized

NOW

❏ Gather your CDs together in one room—don't forget those in the car!
❏ Make Keep, Donate, and Sell piles
❏ Decide whether you want your CDs to be on display
❏ Throw away cassettes if you no longer have a tape deck
❏ Start a catalog of the CDs in your collection
❏ Back up your music collection
❏ Listen to and label all blank CDs

MONTHLY

❏ Organize your existing music collection before adding to it
❏ Create playlists in iTunes or Windows Media Player
❏ Make sure all music files have artist names and track titles
❏ Listen to older CDs to see if you want to keep them

YEARLY

❏ Purchase singles instead of albums until you know you like the artist

Purse & Wallet

Even the smallest handbags have a tendency to become portable medicine cabinets and makeup bags. Limiting what goes into your purse and wallet is key to keeping them organized.

quick start tip

Dump and restock

The first step to getting your purse or wallet in order is to empty and sort the contents. Throw away old lipsticks, empty wrappers, and other unnecessary items. Restock your wallet or purse with fresh items that are usable and clean—and refrain from treating your bag like a trash receptacle in the future.

Edit
your keychain

Are you carrying around the keys to your old gym locker, a padlock you can't locate, and an apartment you no longer live in? This makes finding your house or mail key a frustrating task on a daily basis. Simplify your life by editing a bulky keychain. Toss useless keys in the trash and keep only the keys you use every week on your keyring.

➔ Match your bag or wallet to your lifestyle

Do you need to carry both personal and corporate credit cards? Must your purse double as a briefcase? Do you have kids who are always asking for gum and tissues? Are you constantly searching for your ringing cell phone? Do you carry a digital camera on a daily basis?

Select a bag or wallet based on your needs; one with zippered compartments, small and large pouches and pockets, and a leash to secure keys means never having to dig around again.

Simplify life with a
purse organizer

A purse organizer is a good option if you carry many items in your purse. One such organizer is the Purse Pleaser, which offers separate storage compartments that fit inside any sized handbag. There are spots for your cell phone, wallet, makeup, and keys. Most items stand up for instant visibility and accessibility. Another product to consider is the Purseket. The Purseket is a removable cloth liner with up to 8 storage pouches. Like the Purse Pleaser, the Purseket also keeps items upright and separate—and comes in small, medium, or large.

Purge your purse or wallet

Keep only what you need so you can find everything in a pinch. Every so often, go through your purse and wallet pockets and weed out receipts, empty gift cards, sandwich and coffee punch cards, expired insurance cards, and business cards you no longer need.

Try This!

Get a personal digital assistant like an iPhone or a Blackberry. This one device can reduce your need to tote around pens, paper, business cards, photos, a camera, a day planner, and other bulky items in your bag.

Keep It Organized

NOW

- ❏ Collect loose coins and put them in a change purse
- ❏ Create a list of must-haves for what goes in your bag and wallet
- ❏ Purchase a purse with an attached cell phone holder
- ❏ Hang a purse organizer in your closet to organize your handbags
- ❏ Donate old purses or wallets that you never use
- ❏ Stock your most frequently used purses with your must-haves so you don't forget anything when you switch purses

MONTHLY

- ❏ Dump out the contents of your purse or wallet and reorganize it
- ❏ Add contact information from business cards to your cell phone and then throw out the cards
- ❏ Keep updated photos on your cell phone or get a digital keychain

YEARLY

- ❏ Purchase a new purse or wallet that suits your changing needs

Photos

In your lifetime you will collect thousands of photographs, many of which will end up forgotten, languishing in drawers, envelopes, or in online folders. Take care of your precious memories by implementing a photo filing system that both displays and protects them.

quick start tip

Gather and sort your photos

Make it your first priority to collect all loose photographs from around your house. Include those on your refrigerator and stuffed into drawers. Sort photos into Keep, Toss, and Giveaway piles. Put rubber bands around each pile to keep pictures together until you are ready to deal with them. Preserve them in moisture-proof bins rather than shoe boxes.

Only print your best pictures

Digital cameras make it easy to save every shot and come away from an event with hundreds of photos. But a lot of these images are blurry, poorly composed, or duplicates of other shots. As you sort through your digital pictures, give each one a grade. Then, keep your photo clutter to a minimum by printing and making albums out of only your best, or "A," photos.

➲ Double your efforts with a picture party

Doubles take up a lot of space and are rarely needed. But it hurts to throw doubles away, too. Give doubles a second life by inviting friends or family who are featured in the pictures over for a "doubles picture party."

Ask your guests to bring spare doubles of photos over to trade. Buy a few inexpensive photo albums and give them out at your picture party so people can make albums on the spot.

Put pictures in
albums right away

Photographs pile up and become disorganized when they are left to sit too long. Commit to putting pictures into albums as soon as they are printed. Start by spreading photos out on your dining room table. Write the date, event, and names or places on the back of each photograph and then put them in an album. Stock up on albums when they are on sale so you always have a spare album to put pictures in. Or, consider putting prints in storage and uploading photos from your computer to a digital photo frame—many hold up to 1,000 pictures.

Make digital photo albums

Storing images digitally makes organizing your pictures fast and easy—and saves space in your home. Create online photo albums using programs such as Kodak Easy Share, Flickr, Shutterfly, Picasa, or Snapfish. Name and date each album, create captions for further description, and email them to friends and family.

Try This!

Organize photos in small albums instead of large ones. It can be daunting to put a whole year's worth of photos in one album. Instead, put photos from one event or weekend in 30- to 60-picture albums. This way you can put photos in albums without dealing with all the other pictures you've taken that year.

Keep It Organized

NOW

❑ Throw away blurry prints
❑ Collect loose pictures from around the house and office
❑ Select a few prints to put in frames and mail doubles to friends and family
❑ Schedule a picture party
❑ Organize digital photos into albums or folders
❑ Back up digital images on a memory stick or external hard drive

MONTHLY

❑ Upload photos to an online hosting site for permanent storage
❑ Email online photo albums to friends and family
❑ Make one album with the month's photos

YEARLY

❑ Upgrade your online photo storage capacity
❑ Update framed photos in your home and office
❑ Mail extra photos with your holiday cards

Car

For the less organized among us, our car functions as a traveling living room or a moving storage unit. Keep your car clean and organized by making sure items that are not auto-related are kept out of it.

quick start tip

Keep a small trash bag in your car

Trash builds up in cars because we have no good place to put it. Keep a small bag in your car for refuse. Always keep the bag in the same easily accessible spot so you do not have to search for it. Toss empty water or soda bottles, food wrappers, receipts, and old sets of driving directions in the bag and empty it at least once a week—more if it contains any food items.

Secure bags with a
cargo tote or crate

It is frustrating to get home from the grocery store to find your bags have tipped over on your trip. Unsecured bags result in broken eggs, fruit rolling and rotting beneath a seat, or spilled liquids. Try putting your bags in a cargo tote, which stores them upright against high edges and keeps them from tipping. Or, keep empty milk crates in your trunk to secure bags and other loose items during transit.

➔ Keep kids contained

Prevent a mess before it happens by packing your kids' snacks, drinks, books, portable DVD players, toys, and games in backseat organizers that hang from front seats. There are several models to choose from in many different sizes. Teach your children the proper pocket for each item they take out, as well as what goes in the trash bag. Teach them that backseat organizers aren't the place for wrappers and empty juice boxes.

Create a wiser visor

Cars often double as CD graveyards—loose CDs end up rolling under seats or getting stuffed into armrests or the glove compartment. Keep your CDs neat and easily accessible with a CD organizer that attaches to your visor. Most can hold up to 20 CDs in slots that are easy to reach while driving. CD organizers are also great for storing your insurance card, registration, and other important vehicle information if your glove compartment is too small or messy.

Stow seasonal items

Consider what you need in your car for the current season and put the rest in storage. For example, in winter you may need an ice scraper; during the spring you will need an umbrella handy; and in the summer, you may want a beach towel in the trunk for impromptu daytrips. Storing seasonal items will open up trunk space and leave the nooks and cubbies in your car clutter-free.

Try This!

Tack 5 minutes on to each car trip. Messes pile up in cars when we are rushed and feel like we don't have time to collect trash and find a garbage can. If you make a habit to get where you're going 5 minutes early, you will always have a few minutes free to clean out your car before too much mess accumulates.

Keep It Organized

NOW

❏ Store an envelope in the glove box to collect gas receipts
❏ Put a trash receptacle in your car
❏ Wash your car and vacuum the floor and seats
❏ Put updated insurance and registration information in your glove box
❏ Create a car maintenance schedule and stick to it
❏ Sign up for roadside assistance with AAA or a similar organization
❏ Collect items that don't belong in your car and bring them in your home

MONTHLY

❏ Empty out and organize your glove box and other in-car containers
❏ Determine which seasonal items belong in your car and which can be stored
❏ Check fluid levels—oil, window washer, antifreeze, etc.

YEARLY

❏ Schedule the appointments on your car's maintenance plan

Athletic Gear

Organizing athletic gear is a cinch once you devise a system that works best for your family. One idea is to create sports' stations complete with all gear needed to play a particular sport. Another option is to keep like objects together—for example, storing balls all in one place.

quick start tip

Get your equipment off the floor

Include walls, closets, and the ceiling in your plan to get sports gear off the floor. Use hooks, bags, racks, and shelves to maximize even the smallest space. Storing athletic gear "up" makes it easy to keep track of your equipment—and to find what you need without creating a mess. It also helps preserve the life of your athletic gear.

Use a Rubbermaid
Sports Organizer

If your kids drop their sports gear in the hallway, invest in a Rubbermaid Sports Organizer. At $40, it is a cheap, comprehensive solution to disorganized gear. It is equipped to hold bats, tennis rackets, and hockey sticks upright. The bottom shelf has a cinchable mesh bag in which to store balls, and the top shelf is perfect for storing pads, gloves, and helmets.

➲ Fill stackable crates with small athletic gear

Use multicolored, stackable crates to store small, loose sports items. Assign a color to each of your children—and one to you and your partner—and keep a set of crates in the den, utility room, garage, or basement. Store your family's balls, gloves, helmets, cleats, mouth guards, and other items in nearby crates. Face crates out for easy access. Reserve an empty crate to collect items that have been used and need to be put away.

Make your garage
home base for gear

If you have a garage, make it home base for as much of your sports equipment as possible. Hang kayaks, surfboards, and other large items from the garage ceiling. Use peg boards with heavy-duty hooks to hang helmets, bats, hula hoops, Frisbees, rackets, skates, and even bicycles. Put a shoe rack beneath the peg board to keep your family's athletic shoes all in one place. Use an old armoire to house tennis rackets, hockey sticks, and other oddly shaped equipment.

Go mesh!

Mesh bags are perfect for keeping balls together in one place and make toting them back and forth to the field much easier. Some mesh bags come divided by level, making it easy to keep soccer balls from tennis balls. Most hang easily from ceilings or in corners. Stock up on a few and use extras for laundry bags or stuffed animal storage.

Try This!

Buy, sell, and trade used athletic gear at secondhand sports stores. Stores like Play-It-Again Sports sell high-quality, gently used gear at great prices. You can also trade in your used gear for store credit. Secondhand sports stores help you save money and clear out old equipment from your house.

Keep It Organized

NOW

❏ Repair or throw away broken sports equipment
❏ Donate items your family no longer uses
❏ Rent a locker at your gym and buy a padlock for it
❏ Stock up on plastic crates and mesh bags
❏ Hang a sports organizer in your children's closets
❏ Sell unused gear at a garage sale or sports resale store
❏ Store a first aid kid with your sports equipment
❏ Register bikes with the fire and police departments in case they are stolen

MONTHLY

❏ Check the condition of your athletic gear
❏ Put away seasonal items that aren't in use
❏ Pump up bicycle tires and check seat heights on kids' bikes

YEARLY

❏ Reorganize the garage to accommodate new athletic gear
❏ Have a garage sale to get rid of unused equipment

Electronics

The electronics business is a multimillion-dollar industry because people always want to upgrade to the hottest new gadget. Make responsible choices as you reorganize by upgrading to energy-efficient electronics and recycling obselete models.

quick start tip

Buy all-in-one electronics

Most homes have a television, DVD player, VCR, stereo, and one or more video game systems. There are ways to condense these systems into one or two units. For example, Sony's Playstation 3 system includes gaming, Blu-ray and DVD capability, and Internet access, as well as video, picture, and music storage.

Conceal
electronics and cords

Get a clean, minimalist look by concealing your cable box, receiver, DVD player, VCR, and video game system in a media console. Choose one sturdy enough to support your TV and with clear or frosted-glass panels so you can use your remote right through the cabinets. Look for a console with back openings so your cords slide through and stay hidden away.

⊙ Get a flat screen television

Flat screen televisions create an impressive home theater and also conserve living room space.

Models come with either LCD or plasma screens—both of which produce stunning, high-quality images. Flat screen TVs can be mounted on the wall to free up floor space and allow you to use a smaller media storage unit. Since flat screen TVs consume up to three times more energy than older models, buy one that meets the federal guidelines for the Energy Star program.

Mount speakers
on the wall

Speakers take up a lot of space and add extra wires to your electronics bundle. Depending on how old your speakers are, your best option may be to get rid of them altogether and upgrade to a more modern system. Save up for several small wireless speakers to mount on walls throughout your home. Position speakers in a circle around each room for surround-sound enjoyment.

Do more with your laptop or computer

If buying new electronics is not in your budget, learn to do more with less. Use your laptop to watch DVDs and online TV shows instead of buying a new DVD player or TV. Laptops can be plugged directly into some televisions to watch files on a larger screen. You can also use your laptop or computer as a stereo by plugging speakers into the headphone jack.

Try This!

Technology changes daily. What seemed like the hottest item to you last month may not even make it onto your wish list this month. Wait two months before buying a new electronic device to keep from acquiring things you don't need. After a two-month wait, if you still want the item, go for it.

Keep It Organized

NOW

❑ Remove knick knacks from on top of your electronics
❑ Clean screens with cleansers made for LCD or plasma displays
❑ Get one all-purpose remote for your TV, VCR, DVD, and stereo
❑ Buy Velcro, clips, and other cord organizing products
❑ Use a surge protector
❑ Donate old electronics that still work and recycle broken ones

MONTHLY

❑ Clean and dust all electronics
❑ Track your utility bills and look for ways to cut energy use
❑ Inspect older electronics for worn wires
❑ Research electronics before purchasing using Consumer Reports

YEARLY

❑ Upgrade to electronics that meet federal Energy Star program guidelines
❑ Find out if your utility company offers discounts for greener electronics

Stored Items

Organize storage ideas on paper first. For example, if one of your goals is to easily access Halloween decorations, make a list of items you want accessible and ideas for how to store them. Do this for all stored items and use it as your blueprint.

quick start tip

Be willing to part with possessions

Assess all of the items you currently store and then note the last time you used or even looked at them. Admit that—with certain exceptions—most of what you store is unnecessary. Then become unafraid to part with up to one-third of stored belongings to reduce clutter and streamline your storage project.

Outfit cabinets
with Lazy-Susans

Every cabinet has items that get shoved to the back and forgotten about. Keep these items in rotation by installing Lazy-Susans in your cabinets and pantry. Lazy-Susan turntables come in many sizes and styles to accommodate any budget and taste. Use them in the kitchen to store spices, canned goods, cereal, and storage containers. Use them in the bathroom or hall closet to organize medications, first-aid items, toiletries, and hair products.

➔ Create layers of storage

Organize stored items in layers to conserve space and maximize accessibility.

House items in stackable plastic bins and place them on top of each other, with the heaviest bin on the bottom. Make the most of storage shelf units by placing your most frequently accessed items at eye level. Finally, put items that are used once a year or less towards the back of your storage space.

Preserve, label
and catalog stored items

When storing your belongings, make every effort to preserve the quality of each item. After all, if your stored items are not well cared for, what is the point of storing them? Avoid storing photographs in rooms with dramatic temperature variations or with high humidity, such as basements or attics. Protect your valuables in airtight containers. Once stored, label containers with contents and date stored. Number each bin and create an Excel spreadsheet that catalogs the contents of your stored items.

Set aside space for deep storage

There are certain items you cannot part with but will never use again. These items need a dedicated spot in deep storage. Set aside space in your closet, garage, basement, attic, or spare room for such special belongings. Examples include wedding attire, yearbooks, and certain family heirlooms. Store items in airtight storage bins and keep them out of direct light.

Rent storage space if your home is not big enough to store all your belongings. Renting storage space frees up your home for the things you use every day. Plus, paying for storage will force you to evaluate how badly you want to hang on to old possessions.

Keep It Organized

NOW

❏ Schedule a day to go through stored items
❏ Go through one or two boxes a day until you have examined every one
❏ Set aside a pile for donations
❏ Downsize your belongings to essentials
❏ Leave room for new acquisitions
❏ List items you are not willing to part with
❏ Stock up on storage bins, Space Bags, Sharpies, tape, and labels
❏ Have clothes cleaned before you put them in storage

MONTHLY

❏ Rotate holiday and seasonal items in and out of storage
❏ Ask yourself if you really need an item before putting it in storage
❏ Tell adult children to collect their belongings

YEARLY

❏ Have a garage sale

Conclusion

Congratulations!

By reading *Secrets to Get Organized in Minutes*
you have taken the first step toward putting
your life in order. Because the guesswork has been taken
out of how to organize everything from your receipts to your
basement, you should have a clear idea for how to proceed
today, as well as on a monthly and yearly basis. Now that
you have a plan of action and checklists of tips, organizing
even the most chaotic components of your life should no
longer feel impossible. As American songwriter Joan Baez
once put it, "Action is the antidote to despair." Like with
any major project, however, reorganizing your life and time,
home, important documents, and possessions requires that
you make time to implement your plan.

Secrets to Get Organized in Minutes
includes tips for people with extra free
time as well as those with impossibly
hectic schedules. The topics are broken
down to accommodate everyone from
moms-on-the-go to executives and

college students. In other words, these suggestions will work for anyone who is ready to take control of their chaos! Even the busiest reader should feel motivated and inspired by the Quick Start Tips and valuable ideas throughout this book.

These tips are succinct and give clear direction for how to take action and get immediate results. Note and enjoy the wonderful progress you make after enacting them. Your success will serve as encouragement to tackle the bigger challenges in the organization process. Remember, becoming—and remaining—an organized person is realistic, simple, and entirely possible once you break your lifestyle down into manageable categories.

Above all, stay focused on the big picture— the many benefits of being organized to your life. The organized life includes reduced stress; fewer conflicts with roommates, your spouse, and family; and more time and

energy. You will be amazed at how much you enjoy spending time in your home once you have implemented just one chapter's worth of suggestions from this book. You may host your very first dinner party for friends, or enjoy an evening with your family in your newly organized living room. You will feel stress melt away with your clutter.

Congratulations on taking the first step toward your newly organized home and life!